Especially for

....

From

....

Date

....

beautiful garden

How
God Grows
a
Woman
of Confidence

A Devotional

Anita Higman &
Judy Gordon Morrow

BARBOUR BOOKS
An Imprint of Barbour Publishing, Inc.

Published by Barbour Books, an imprint of Barbour Publishing, Inc., 1810 Barbour Drive, Uhrichsville, Ohio 44683, www.barbourbooks.com

Our mission is to inspire the world with the life-changing message of the Bible.

Member of the
Evangelical Christian
Publishers Association

Printed in China.

To my longtime editor friends
at Barbour Publishing—
Kelly McIntosh and Annie Tipton.
Thank you for your fine support
and your tireless efforts to spread
the Good News of Jesus Christ!
You're both an inspiration!

Anita Higman

For my precious granddaughters,
Michelle and Camille
Mylee
Adya and Elowen,
with my prayers that you will always
enjoy sweet confidence in Jesus Christ.
He loves you so much, and so do I!

"Grandma Judy"
Judy Gordon Morrow

Introduction

According to the world's wisdom, we should automatically feel like confident women empowered for greatness. Yes, supermoms with cool style, sassy hair, and killer accessories—while simultaneously swinging like Jane through the jungles of commerce. We become convinced we must fight to do life our way and demand our day in the sun.

Whew! Secretly you're thinking, *How can I possibly do all that when I need a medieval catapult just to hoist myself out of bed in the morning?*

But according to the Bible and the God who made you, you were never ever meant to do it alone.

So, take heart. Let your shoulders relax, your spirit unwind, and have another cup of coffee with the Lord. Grow and delight in Christ's all-powerful presence. Treasure His challenges, direction, and encouragements. Praise Him and thank Him for all that He is and for all that He will do. Bask in His light and love, and *then* do life, because with Christ by your side, you can do all things!

Now *that* is a hope and truth we can all wake up to!

Les lepidopteres ... d'ordre d'insectes d...
(imago) ... appelée ...

...beautiful garden

Many butterflies use camouflage,
mimicry and aposematism
to evade their predators.

The Invisibles

*Therefore encourage one another and
build each other up, just as in fact you are doing.*
1 Thessalonians 5:11

Have you ever felt invisible? Not the cool superhero kind, but the kind that gets trampled because no one is paying attention?

There seems to be a world of people out there who are lonely, depressed, and feeling sort of "too small" to be seen by the rest of humanity. No one appears to care if they succeed or fail, laugh or cry, live or die.

How is it that we find ourselves—even as Christians—in such a predicament, so discouraged? As part of the body of Christ, we need to remember that we are to lift one another up. We are to encourage one another. How? By telling others how much they are appreciated and necessary. By not taking on all the jobs in the body but allowing others to shine with their many God-given gifts too. By overlooking faults and leaving our judgments and criticisms behind. By simply loving others as Christ has loved us.

Helping someone else feel confident in Christ is one way for us to become confident in the Lord; because as we help others, we too are encouraged until our cup is running over!

*Lord, help me to remember that tearing down the body of
believers or making them feel left out is not Your intention.
Instead, help me to remember to be an encourager! Amen. —A.H.*

This Marvelous Place

"There are many homes up there where my Father lives,
and I am going to prepare them for your coming. When everything
is ready, then I will come and get you, so that you can always be
with me where I am. If this weren't so, I would tell you plainly."
JOHN 14:3 TLB

You have cleaned until the house sparkles. You have prepared food that is fit for a king. You have put down a fresh bouquet of lavender for the pillow, and you've thought of everything imaginable to make your guest feel not only at home and welcome but also filled with every manner of delight. In other words, you have a beloved guest coming, and a grand celebration is about to commence.

And oh how much grander and finer will be that day when we arrive in heaven. The Lord has made us promises, and because He has kept His other divine promises, He will fulfill the rest.

That is something to boost our confidence today and all the rest of the days of our lives.

Thank You, Father God, that You made a way for me to be with
You for all time. I look forward to this marvelous place You have
prepared for me. In Jesus' name I pray. Amen. —A.H.

On Wings like Eagles

But those who hope in the LORD
will renew their strength.
They will soar on wings like eagles;
they will run and not grow weary,
they will walk and not be faint.
ISAIAH 40:31

An eagle spreads its broad wings wide, which allows it to catch the warm currents of air that rise from the earth. These birds fly higher and higher, soaring miles above the earth. How glorious to witness that majestic glide on high. And what a powerful image for us as Christians.

But when we take our hope and place it with the world, we will grow weary with despair. Our hard work will go nowhere; our love will not flourish as it should. We will stumble and faint from all the wild, frantic trying.

When we place our hope in the Lord, we will renew our strength no matter what happens. We can fulfill our purpose. And we can do it with dignity and grace and power because we are going to the source of all power and might, the fount of all wisdom, the supplier of all goodness and love.

Yes, oh yes, we will soar on wings like eagles!

Dear God, may we take that majestic glide together.
I put my hope in You. In Jesus' name I pray. Amen. —A.H.

A Cluttered Soul

*"So if you are presenting your offering at the altar,
and while there you remember that your brother has something
[such as a grievance or legitimate complaint] against you, leave your
offering there at the altar and go. First make peace with your
brother, and then come and present your offering."*

MATTHEW 5:23–24 AMP

Okay, dinner is ready, and boy does it look fine! The heavenly smell of roast with potatoes as well as homemade apple pie is romancing its ways through your senses. Your taste buds are ready to do a tango.

But as you sit down to your gloriously prepared meal, you see a pile of papers and junk mail strewn on the sides of your kitchen table. Then you notice some dust kitties and trash on the floor. Sort of ruins the atmosphere for your fine dining experience!

And so it is with the cluttered soul.

If we come to the Lord with our time, talent, or treasure, and all the while we have wronged a sister in Christ, then wouldn't that taint our gifts and hinder any kind of intimacy with the Lord? Let peacemaking be our watchword as we live our lives before God and humanity. Then our loving offerings to Christ and our communion with Him will be as it should be.

*Lord, I admit I have wronged my friend. I will go to
her and make things right. Thank You for showing me
the way to please You in all things. Amen. —A.H.*

Muddy Moments

*Casting all your cares [all your anxieties, all your worries,
and all your concerns, once and for all] on Him, for He cares about
you [with deepest affection, and watches over you very carefully].*

1 PETER 5:7 AMP

When Easter draws close, you're not only preparing your heart for this miracle holiday, you're going to have a bit of fun coloring eggs. You line up your little vats of dye, and you begin the process of transforming mere chicken eggs into pastel delights. But just as you wind up your amusements, you can't help but pour all the dye colors together to see what other hue you might come up with. As always, the egg comes out a muddy, blah color that has no name but ugly.

Why do we pour the colors together when we know the outcome? Could be just a case of the sillies. But it is a curious habit of many Easter egg dippers. Maybe it's because we accept on some deeper level that life will not only give us pretty moments but also the hard-boiled kind—the muddy, blah moments that have no name but ugly.

When that happens, remember that God cares about both the pretty moments and the ugly ones. Go to Him with whatever you have. He cares about you with the deepest affection and watches over you very carefully!

*Thank You, Lord, that I can come to You with all
my life, no matter what it looks like. Amen. —A.H.*

The Heavens Tell of Your Glory

The heavens are telling the glory of God;
they are a marvelous display of his craftsmanship.

PSALM 19:1 TLB

It's springtime—hooray!—and there is this heavenly grove of winged elm trees that you pass by on your evening walks. In the winter months, you can easily see the flat-winged shape of some of the branches—so ancient-looking and artistic. But in the spring when the slightly weeping, peach-tipped leaves bud out, you are amazed all over again. A breeze puffs through the branches, and the waving effect makes the feathery fronds seem as if the tree has been hosting a flock of leafy birds, which are now taking off into the great blue yonder!

Oh, how creative is our God. His workmanship is like none other. He is most worthy of our awe and adoration! To intimately know and worship such a Creator God should give us great hope and assurance as we walk through our days!

Mighty Maker of heaven and earth, all of life shouts of Your glory. I worship and adore You for all that You have created for us to enjoy! As I rush through my busy days, may I never take You for granted or any of Your marvelous creation. In Jesus' name I pray. Amen. —A.H.

That Chic New Look

So roll up your sleeves, put your mind in gear, be totally ready to receive the gift that's coming when Jesus arrives. Don't lazily slip back into those old grooves of evil, doing just what you feel like doing. You didn't know any better then; you do now. As obedient children, let yourselves be pulled into a way of life shaped by God's life, a life energetic and blazing with holiness. God said, "I am holy; you be holy."
1 PETER 1:13–16 MSG

As you ready yourself for another day of work, you gaze into the mirror and think, *Wow, not so great. I need to update my look.* So you go in search of the coolest blazer, the sassiest heels, and the chicest jewelry to accessorize!

Nothing wrong with looking groomed and graceful, but it can become quite the treadmill. We look and feel good until the bangles break, the shoes go out of style, and that blazer gets blammo-ed with a spaghetti stain!

Need a beauty makeover that lasts? Want to be cool and confident when you gaze in the mirror? Ask Christ to re-dress your spirit so that you will have an energetic life that is blazing with holiness. Be assured, the Lord would love to do that very thing!

Lord, I am ready for Your spiritual makeover.
I am excited to be all You created me to be. Amen. —A.H.

Bull in a China Shop

*Jesus, full of the Holy Spirit, left the Jordan
and was led by the Spirit into the wilderness.*
LUKE 4:1

If you leave a bull in a dainty china shop long enough, it's only a matter of time before there's going to be trouble. That bull will swing wide with his thundering frame and a display of crystal ornaments will be history. Maybe he'll charge into a stack of fine china and transform it into a heap of broken glass. Even swishing his tale might topple a delicate vase.

Do you ever feel clumsy like that bull—perhaps in your relationships? At home or church, in your marriage, with your kids, and in some friendships? You just feel like no matter what you do or say, it comes out as unwieldy as that bull swinging wide? You hurt someone with a misunderstanding. You meant good, but it came out badly. You told the truth in love, but you broke someone's heart in the process. You feel you've left an emotional pile of rubble in your wake.

Okay, so life is clunky, and the last thing you feel is confident. What to do?

Pray that the Holy Spirit will lead you daily. In your words, your actions, and in your deeds. That His divine touch will be evident in all that you do.

*Holy Spirit, help me in all my comings and goings.
Teach me the way I should go. May I put my
confidence in Your daily guidance. Amen. —A.H.*

FOMO

One acronym that has currently found its way into our society is FOMO, which is a fear of missing out. The root of this anxiety comes from obsessively connecting to techno gadgets and social media. This fear sounds modern, but in some ways it's as old as humanity. Ever since humans fell from grace and were banished from the Garden of Eden, we have lived with this underlying terror that we are missing out on something big. Well, because we *are*! The day Adam and Eve chose rebellion, we lost our intimate connection with the Almighty.

So where is the hope? Well, as far as FOMO—disconnect from time to time from the artificial realm of gadgets and social media, and then plug in to more real one-on-one chats and experiences with friends and family. You will find your way back to a calmer mind-set and a healthier life. So, then, what is the answer for missing out on paradise lost and our close fellowship with God? We can plug in to the best connection we will ever know—and that is the saving power of Jesus Christ.

*Lord, thank You that when You are by my side, I'm confident
that I'm not missing out on anything important. I know Your Holy
Spirit will guide me into all that is best for me. Amen. —A.H.*

All the Time in the World

*"He will wipe every tear from their eyes, and
there will be no more death or sorrow or crying
or pain. All these things are gone forever."*

REVELATION 21:4 NLT

We live in a high-speed, hurry-up-and-wait, frantic kind of world. So much so that we can barely finish a conversation. We can barely complete a task. We can barely breathe.

Take heart. We are promised in God's Word that, as Christians, we have the promise and hope of heaven. We will not only know everlasting joy, but we will also have more than enough time for all things because time will know no end. Imagine how that will be—to have all the time in the world for everything we've ever dreamed of! The luxury of time for what is wondrous, what is beautiful. Time to create, to know, to travel, to visit, to laugh, to ponder. To love, to study, to solve some of the mysteries of the universe. To worship and commune with the very One who made us—made you.

Oh yes, just imagine!

*Thank You, Lord, for the glory of heaven. When the world
threatens to steal all my hope, my confidence, and my smile,
I can rest in the knowledge that someday we will have
all the time in the world together. Amen. —A.H.*

Here's the Joy!

*For it is by grace you have been saved, through faith—
and this is not from yourselves, it is the gift of God—
not by works, so that no one can boast.*

EPHESIANS 2:8–9

Ever feel exhausted spiritually? Is it because people are demanding you do more as a Christian? You must strive more, sacrifice more, struggle more, give more—until you feel you are under the burden of a false religion rather than under the grace of God. Satan would like nothing better than to make you feel that being a follower of Christ is too impossible to achieve. But Christianity is a relationship, not a religion. There are no works good enough or sacrifices perfect enough or worldly disciplines stringent enough to get you into heaven. Following Christ is about being with Him daily in a real and intimate relationship.

Yes, may we always walk closely with our Lord and enjoy doing good deeds for our fellow man, but only out of a grateful response to Christ's mercy, love, and redemption—not with the mind-set that anything we strive to do will get us into heaven. So embrace the truth, the simplicity, the love. Here lies the freedom, the rest. Here lies the joy!

*Lord, I accept Your free and perfect gift of salvation,
and I joyfully go out into the world with confidence
as I share this Good News! Amen. —A.H.*

The Lion of Judah

Ever watch the evening news and want to hide? Ever get on social media and you no longer recognize your friends—that is, the same ones who used to share recipes with each other are now sharing vitriol against each other? Ever wonder what happened to communities that worked together? Love that had no strings? Friends who gave each other the benefit of the doubt? Some days do you feel so riddled with fear that you want to give up?

The Word of God can be such a refuge in times of earthly travail. In the book of Revelation, our Lord is referred to as the Lion of Judah. We are worshipping and relying on and being empowered by a God who is invincible and omnipotent, so we have every reason to fulfill the command that says to be strong and full of courage. With the Lord by our side, we do not need to be terrified or dismayed or intimidated by what happens around us in this fallen world. Take heart, the Lord God (the Lion of Judah) will go with us wherever we go.

This is our promise. This is our daily hope.

*Lord Jesus, thank You for reminding me that with You
by my side I can live a life of courage! Amen. —A.H.*

Ready for a Meltdown

So God blessed the seventh day and made it holy, because on it God rested from all his work that he had done in creation.
GENESIS 2:3 ESV

You whirl through your days, and in order to keep up with everything on your to-do list, you have begun to multitask. You have begun to drive a little faster. Okay, a lot faster. You have put off your friends and family. You have given up quiet time, prayer time, and Bible-reading time. But no matter how you bustle and elbow your way through your days, you just can't keep up.

Yes, you're locked and loaded for a meltdown.

It's hard to face the world with confidence when you're in a constant state of churning chaos. The world might admonish you by telling you to get your act together, but God would advise the opposite. Rest. Take Sunday off each week, and luxuriate in the quiet beauty of it. Soak up the Son-shine. Seek the Lord, and find Him—He wants to commune with you. Relish that time with Him. Be refreshed and restored. And find yourself ready for Monday morning. Yes, start the new week confident in Christ and in the good plans He has for you!

Dearest Lord Jesus, I am looking forward to some serious downtime on Sundays. Time to rest with my friends and family. Time to pause and ponder. And most important, time to be with You! Amen. —A.H.

A Promise We Can Embrace

*And a crowd was sitting around him, and they said to him,
"Your mother and your brothers are outside, seeking you."
And he answered them, "Who are my mother and my brothers?"
And looking about at those who sat around him, he said,
"Here are my mother and my brothers! For whoever does
the will of God, he is my brother and sister and mother."*

MARK 3:32–35 ESV

It's easy for people to say they really want to do the will of God. But if that meant they had to give up a closely held dream, a lifestyle, wealth, or anything else dearly cherished, would they still mean those words with all their hearts and souls?

And yet to do the will of God is the highest calling. It's *the* mission and passion of a lifetime. The Bible goes further. Jesus said, "For whoever does the will of God, he is my brother and sister and mother."

Amazing, right? Seems too good to be true, and yet it is a promise we can embrace and rejoice in! Nothing in this life could be better than that.

*I thank You, Lord, that because I want to follow in
Your footsteps and do Your will, I am called Your
sister. I love that. I love You! Amen. —A.H.*

I Have This Mountain, Lord

Jesus replied, "Truly I tell you, if you have faith and do not doubt, not only can you do what was done to the fig tree, but also you can say to this mountain, 'Go, throw yourself into the sea,' and it will be done."
MATTHEW 21:21

What is your mountain today? Chronic pain? An unruly child who refuses to obey even the smallest request? A neighbor who makes a sport out of annoying you on a daily basis? A job that doesn't pay nearly enough to cover your most basic bills? A broken vow that leaves you feeling abandoned and plummeting into depression?

God is there with you in every kind of earthly distress. Ask Him to come to your rescue. He may not move that mountain using your time schedule or He may not answer your prayer in the way you expect, but He does care for you, and He will answer you. He will indeed work things out for your good because you love Him. When all the rest of the world falls away from you in unfaithfulness and falsehood, God is faithful. God is love.

As it reminds us in Hebrews 10:23, "Let us hold fast the confession of our hope without wavering, for he who promised is faithful" (ESV).

Thank You, Lord, for being faithful in moving my mountains. In Jesus' name I pray. Amen. —A.H.

A Forgery of Faith

Beloved, do not believe every spirit [speaking through a self-proclaimed prophet]; instead test the spirits to see whether they are from God, because many false prophets and teachers have gone out into the world.

1 John 4:1 amp

If you are confused in your faith or question the wisdom of some of the precepts preached in your church, you might consider the idea that you may have embraced a forgery of faith. There is nothing new in this, since false teachings happened even in biblical times.

One could say that false prophets equal a false confidence. You might not know you've gone adrift, which makes the situation even more spiritually hazardous.

How can one test the spirits, then, as it says to do in 1 John? If you find yourself following a belief system or teaching that puts an emphasis on man and not God, flee from it. If it pulls you away from the Lord or the Bible, or if the teaching doesn't honor Christ as the Son of God and all that He has accomplished with His death and resurrection, then have no part in it. Stay close to the Lord in prayer, read God's Word to show you what is right and good, seek the counsel of godly men and women, and ask the Holy Spirit to guide you into all truth. God will honor your diligence.

Holy Spirit, give me discernment in my faith. Amen. —A.H.

Mesmerized by Sin

By faith Moses, when he was grown up, refused to be called the son of Pharaoh's daughter, choosing rather to be mistreated with the people of God than to enjoy the fleeting pleasures of sin.
HEBREWS 11:24–25 ESV

It has been said that people can see a tornado and become so mesmerized by the whirling horror of it that they almost don't flee to safety in time to save their own lives. Why do humans do that? Forfeit common sense for an irresistible glimpse at what might be enthralling but equally deadly?

Perhaps that is what Lot's wife felt when she disobeyed the angel and looked back at the city of Sodom and Gomorrah as it was being destroyed by fire and sulfur from heaven. But that one act of defiance turned out to be deadly for her.

And so it goes with sin in our lives. We can get so mesmerized by its shiny and glittery facets that we can easily forget it is about to kill us—body, mind, and soul.

Lord, may I never get so entranced by sin that I get caught up in its whirling dangers. Give me the courage and will to see it for what it is and always break free from it. In Jesus' name I pray. Amen. —A.H.

A Beautiful Balance

*Humble yourselves [with an attitude of repentance
and insignificance] in the presence of the Lord, and He
will exalt you [He will lift you up, He will give you purpose].*

JAMES 4:10 AMP

The world says, "Value yourself." God says, "Humble yourself." The world says, "Be proud." God says, "Repent."

You get the idea. God's ways are not our ways. We come at life from a very different viewpoint, and that "view" usually has us staring in the mirror saying, "Yeah, it really *is* all about me." Even if we don't say the words, sometimes our actions scream that mind-set when we are overly preoccupied with ourselves. That obnoxious attitude is not pleasing to God, and it usually makes people want to run from us.

Does that mean we should despise ourselves and believe we are worthless? No; in God's eyes, we are precious. We are indeed valued. We are loved. We have a purpose. But we are not to bulldoze into the world with a haughty attitude, obsessed with our own lives and our own needs. Egomania isn't in heaven's vocabulary.

So where is the biblical balance?

By staying connected to God. He will not let you fall into pride if you ask Him for a beautiful balance—embracing humility and yet knowing your worth in Christ. Then God promises to exalt you!

*Lord, please lead me in Your humble ways.
In Jesus' name I pray. Amen. —A.H.*

All Is Not Lost

What then shall we say to these things?
If God is for us, who can be against us?
ROMANS 8:31 ESV

Because of some vicious gossip, your coworkers are now avoiding you. You stood up at a local community meeting, you spoke the truth in love, and then you faced a roomful of angry frowns and sharp retorts. You humbly apologized to a dear friend for something you did, and instead of forgiving you, she made the decision to walk away from your longtime friendship. Yes, it's official—that big, beautiful ship of yours that you thought was sailing the waters blue has run aground. You're stuck, and you feel the whole world is on the shore, arms folded tightly, standing against you.

Oh, but all is not lost. Rest in knowing that God is for you. And if God is on your side, you are in the best place there is. You might not have perfect days, but make no mistake, our God stands with you, and He's still in control of all things. Yes, be of good courage. Christ has overcome the world!

Lord, I thank You for loving me, caring for me,
and for standing with me no matter what. I need You.
I love You! In Jesus' name I pray. Amen. —A.H.

The Golden Ball

But if you have bitter jealousy and selfish ambition in your hearts, do not boast and be false to the truth. This is not the wisdom that comes down from above, but is earthly, unspiritual, demonic. For where jealousy and selfish ambition exist, there will be disorder and every vile practice.

JAMES 3:14–16 ESV

Ouch! This scripture from James seems kind of harsh, but the Bible simply speaks truth about the human condition. Who among us can say that we've succeeded daily in being free from any selfish ambition, jealousy, or vain conceit? Many times we've been looking out for ourselves above the needs of others. In fact, the scripture goes on to say that this will bring disorder and every kind of vile practice.

Yes, sometimes we've been handed a golden ball—that is, a thing we long for in this life and cherish deeply—but once we're clutching that golden ball, we don't pass it on like we would in a good game. We don't laugh in camaraderie, and we don't share the glory of a win. We instead become a one-woman game. We cling to the golden ball until our hands ache and our spirits fail us. Because we are meant to share our lives and our gifts—with one another—and with God.

Lord, show me how to share all the gifts You've given me, even what I cherish, and help me to watch out for the needs of others. Amen. —A.H.

The God We Adore

*The heavens declare the glory of God,
and the sky above proclaims his handiwork.*
PSALM 19:1 ESV

You step out into a night sky, and your eyes widen along with your spirit as you take in the majesty of the heavens, God's spectacular points of light. Perhaps this is a physical reminder in His creation that He never leaves us alone, even in the hours of darkness.

A spring storm whirls in, and the gusts and clashing thunder take your breath away. We may shudder at the spectacle, but there is also pleasure in knowing the One who controls all things, including our lives.

You travel to a distant land, and just around a bend in the road you see a vista of hills with a pristine river that meanders through the middle of a green, green valley. Wildflowers dot the landscape along with a few plump and contented cows, but the jewel in the crown on the pastoral scene is the chapel with a steeple and its clear-ringing bells.

Take courage and know this—the God we adore, the One we put our confidence in—is the Creator of all of this. All things good, all things wonderful.

*Creator God, I am in awe of Your pageantry and the home
You created for us called Earth! Thank You! Amen. —A.H.*

The Apple of His Eye

"And I will be a father to you, and you shall be sons and daughters to me, says the Lord Almighty."

2 Corinthians 6:18 esv

It was the little girl's birthday, and what she wanted along with the glittery tiara and fairy-tale princess outfit was to dance with her daddy. Her father—who loved her most dearly—found some enchanting music and tried ardently to make his daughter's birthday wish come true. The father bowed and the little girl curtsied. After placing her wobbly feet on her daddy's big shoes, they took to dancing across the room. They laughed that day. They swirled round and round, and she received the sweetest memories a father could give his daughter. The adults at the party said, "Look at that. Oh, how they love each other. She is the apple of his eye."

And so it goes with you and God. He calls you His daughter and loves you most dearly. You are, in fact, the apple of His eye.

So dance through this life with the confidence of knowing who you are in Christ and just how much you are loved.

I love You, Lord, for making me part of Your family. I am so honored to be Your beloved daughter. In Jesus' name I pray. Amen. —A.H.

When All Seems Lost

*Then they cried to the Lord in their trouble,
and he delivered them from their distress.*

PSALM 107:19 ESV

Hope rose with the dawn, but clouds of despair quickly overshadowed her spirit. Soon she faced the darkest hour of her life. Have you ever felt like this—that life had done its worst? That all you can think to do now is to go into a quiet room and weep tears of anguish? Perhaps what was promised to you long ago was snatched away. Or the person you counted on has turned her back on you. Perhaps your husband went on to heaven—way too young and way too suddenly.

When a cruel life event overpowers you—when all seems lost—do not lose hope. Do not despair. Cry out to the Lord. He is the Great Rescuer. A help in time of trouble.

We have the greatest hope of all—that the One who came to save us is the same One who will someday take us home, where there will be no more hopeless dawns, no more tears of disappointment and despair, and no more death.

*Father God, when I feel all is lost, I'm so grateful
that I can cry out to You. Thank You that Your mercy
endures forever. In Jesus' name I pray. Amen. —A.H.*

Confronted with the Truth

*And they heard the sound of the LORD God walking in the garden
in the cool of the day, and the man and his wife hid themselves
from the presence of the LORD God among the trees of the garden.*

GENESIS 3:8 ESV

More and more Christians—even the beloved and famous ones—seem
to be getting caught in some pretty serious sins. But when they are con-
fronted with the truth, they simply deny it all. They don't seem interested
in true confession or facing the consequences of their sins.

How do humans find themselves in such spiritual binds? Perhaps they
have been in denial for so long that they become delusional, believing
they truly are innocent. Maybe they shrug off the sin, making excuses
and thinking that if everyone else does it, why not? Maybe they think
they deserve it somehow. Perhaps for a season, they do grieve over the
sin but then fall right back into the same dark rut.

When Adam and Eve fell from grace, they hid from God. Unfor-
tunately, that is what we are still doing today. We can't be poised for
service in God's kingdom when we're hiding from our transgressions.
God says to repent. Plain and simple. The Lord is clear. We should be
honest with Him too.

*Lord Jesus, I know I am a sinner, and I confess my failings
to You now. Please forgive me, and set me free. Amen. —A.H.*

The Desires of My Heart

"If you then, who are evil, know how to give good gifts to your children, how much more will your Father who is in heaven give good things to those who ask him!"
MATTHEW 7:11 ESV

There at the top of the staircase is a loose ball of yarn, and when the roly-poly thing takes a tumble down the steps, the great unraveling begins until there is only a nub of a ball left. Is that how it feels when things start going wrong in your life? It's easy to grow cynical after a few hard bounces and after staring at your dream there on the floor, which has been reduced to a worthless scrap. We might then be tempted to make it a habit to consider all the worst possible scenarios in every life situation. We might say things like, "Nothing good will come out of my work, my life. I feel helpless and hopeless."

But none of this kind of thinking or talk will help us. Instead, putting our trust in God is a life changer. We are reminded in Matthew that if we—who can be immoral and malevolent—can give good gifts to our kids, then how much more will our Father in heaven give us good gifts if we ask!

Lord, I trust You with my future, and right now I ask You for the desire of my heart. In Jesus' name I pray. Amen. —A.H.

Swept Off Our Feet

But God, being rich in mercy, because of the great love with which he loved us, even when we were dead in our trespasses, made us alive together with Christ—by grace you have been saved.
EPHESIANS 2:4–5 ESV

Oh, we women love to be loved, eh? But we don't want a puny, little love. No, we want the big, bold, and beautiful kind that doesn't hesitate to say it, to show it, to shout it. We want to be cared for and cherished and maybe even doted on. Yes, we want a man who is attentive to the details of our lives. If you do find yourself rich in love, you dare not ask for the ultimate commitment though. That is, if the need arose, would he come to your rescue and even be willing to give up his own life to save yours? No, you dare not ask such a thing, since it seems like too great a sacrifice. Too much to ask of anyone.

And yet that is the outrageous, beautiful kind of love God offered us through Christ—the very thing we dared not ask of anyone else on earth. Oh my. Yes, we have been officially swept off our feet by the impassioned love of our God.

Have you officially accepted His proposal?

Jesus, thank You for loving me so much that You gave up Your life to save mine. Yes, I choose life with You for all time! Amen. —A.H.

Laughing at the Future

Strength and dignity are her clothing,
and she laughs at the time to come.
PROVERBS 31:25 ESV

Okay, so you've slipped on your rose-colored glasses, but the future still looks like a train wreck. You've prayed about your travails, but then five minutes later you start twisting your palms together. The days are sweaty and the nights are sleepless. You make endless, clever plans to try to outsmart the days and months ahead but to no avail. Then when you finally come to the end of yourself, you come face-to-face with one important truth—the future cannot be controlled. Not by you. Not by anyone. Doesn't matter how young or old you are. How rich or how smart you are.

You can choose to go nuts with worry, or you can truly give it all to God with confidence. Then you can not only rest well, but you can also throw your head back in laughter. Why? Because God made you, He loves you, and He's proved Himself to be trustworthy through the ages.

Yes, laugh. People will either think you're crazy or they'll lean in to listen carefully, hoping to find the one truth that will change their lives forever.

Dearest Lord, You have proved Yourself to be loving
and trustworthy. I surrender all to You. Amen. —A.H.

Thorn in the Flesh

*So to keep me from becoming conceited because of the surpassing
greatness of the revelations, a thorn was given me in the flesh,
a messenger of Satan to harass me, to keep me from becoming
conceited. Three times I pleaded with the Lord about this, that it
should leave me. But he said to me, "My grace is sufficient
for you, for my power is made perfect in weakness."*

2 CORINTHIANS 12:7–9 ESV

Power corrupts. That saying has enough truth in it to make us squirm.
We don't have to be a president or a princess to know the temptation of
pride. It can seep in from anywhere like a toxic gas, making us puff up.
Paul, who could have been made haughty by the many powerful things
God was doing in and through him, was allowed to suffer a harassment
of some kind in his body that made it hard for him to be anything but
real and humble and usable.

And that is exactly what God wants of us.

Do you have a thorn in the flesh? How does God use this weakness
to make His power perfect that you might be usable for His kingdom?
Even though this hardship might be, well, hard, it is also a blessing in
that to be free from an attitude of arrogant self-reliance means our lives
can produce good and nourishing fruit!

*Lord, no matter what, I want to be real
and humble and usable! Amen. —A.H.*

Isn't It Lovely?

*Oil and perfume make the heart glad; so does the
sweetness of a friend's counsel that comes from the heart.*

PROVERBS 27:9 AMP

Isn't it lovely to have a good and godly friend? Someone to come alongside you in difficult times? Someone to laugh with you over life's quirky moments, to grow with, to be inspired by, to eat lunches together, and to grab quick coffees at your favorite haunts? Well, someone to do life with? And on those occasions when you need some good advice, you know she will be loving and honest and will prayerfully help you on your way. That's a friend indeed! It's as sweet as that most beloved perfume you dab on your wrist when you want to feel wonderful.

If you are fortunate enough to be one of those blessed people with a dear friend described in this passage, be sure and tell her today how much she means to you. Maybe you could call her up or take her out to lunch and say, "I am so glad God made you. You are a wonderful addition to this earth and to my life!"

*Thanks, Lord, for creating such a beautiful thing called
friendship, and thank You for being my dearest and
best friend. Oh yes, it is indeed lovely! Amen. —A.H.*

In Good Company

He was despised and rejected by men,
a man of sorrows and acquainted with grief;
and as one from whom men hide their faces
he was despised, and we esteemed him not.
ISAIAH 53:3 ESV

Almost all humans get blue from time to time. And many people suffer from occasional depression for various reasons. It is a common ailment of the spirit, especially now in our modern times with such a serious breakdown in the way our society operates. Basic kindness and decency seem to be mere shadows of a bygone era. But even on good days, people can still struggle with what could be called a grieving of the heart.

Some of the godliest, smartest, and most creative people throughout history have suffered with depression. You are not alone. In fact, you're in good company. Jesus Himself was called a man of sorrows and acquainted with grief. This fallen world is a very hard place to live and work. But in Psalm 34:18, we are lovingly reminded, "The LORD is near to the brokenhearted and saves the crushed in spirit" (ESV). What an endearing promise.

So rest in this safe assurance, and share this glorious hope!

Lord, even when I am feeling downtrodden, I know You
are ever near me. In Jesus' name I pray. Amen. —A.H.

What Will They Say?

Keep your eyes open, hold tight to your convictions,
give it all you've got, be resolute, and love without stopping.
1 CORINTHIANS 16:13–14 MSG

The ancient live oak tree—the one that had many a story to tell from its years of glory—had sadly died. So a team of men came to bring it down piece by piece. The mammoth and once-healthy limbs hit the ground with rocking thunder. Yes, the roots had run deeply, making the branches reach widely to welcome all. The tree had provided good shade for families at the park. Picnics and giggles. The sweet kisses of lovers. Kites getting caught in the branches. The tree even knew a lightning strike once that could have killed it, but it recovered and went on to offer many more opportunities for love and laughter beneath its branches. Some people stood around the tree that day, sad to see it go. But they also remembered the many happy days they'd known beneath its shade.

Humans can be a bit like that old tree. What will people say about you one day? That your roots ran deeply in your faith in the Lord? That you stood strong against injustice and lived a life of integrity? Will they miss you and your welcoming arms and your loving spirit? Will they have pleasant days of remembrance?

Lord, I want my roots of faith in You to be strong. I want
people to remember me as loving greatly. Amen. —A.H.

Mindful of God

"When the LORD your God goes ahead of you and destroys the nations and you drive them out and live in their land, do not fall into the trap of following their customs and worshiping their gods. Do not inquire about their gods, saying, 'How do these nations worship their gods? I want to follow their example.' "
DEUTERONOMY 12:29–30 NLT

There's a new spiritual fad in town called "mindfulness," but really the practice of doing life our own way is as old as time.

God warned the Israelites that they were not to be influenced by other countries that worshipped other gods. We as a nation have a wonderful variety of people from all over the world. As Christians we should love others, defend everyone's freedom of religion, and even celebrate other cultures. But the one thing we are never to do is worship their false gods or be influenced by any of their spiritual practices or disciplines that pertain to their belief system.

And yet just like the Israelites, we have allowed ourselves to be influenced, and we have taken up practices that don't honor God and don't rely on His power for divine help or salvation.

We should flee from all that does not honor our Lord and His work on the cross. We should read the Word of God and pray and stay connected to a Bible-believing church. Be mindful of God and what He wants.

Lord, give me discernment so that
I might always please You. Amen. —A.H.

Come and Rest with Me

Because the Lord is my Shepherd, I have everything I need!
He lets me rest in the meadow grass and leads me beside
the quiet streams. He gives me new strength. He helps
me do what honors him the most.
PSALM 23:1–3 TLB

Are you too harried, too lonely, too fearful to be confident? Yes, that may be you and billions of other people. Too harried because we have taken on too much work, too much busyness, too much volunteering, too much of everything. *"Come and rest with Me,"* He whispers.

Are you lonely because you bought into the lie that all those thousands of friends on social media truly are your intimate friends? And yet we can't possibly keep up with them all, listen to them all, reply to them all. *"Come and rest with Me,"* He whispers.

Are we too fearful? Maybe we also need to take time away from the news that bombards us everywhere we go—cafés, phones, home, computers, virtually everywhere. *"Come and rest with Me,"* He whispers.

Regain your confidence and your strength in the Lord. Go away with Him to the meadows and quiet streams. Rest. Refresh. Rejoice. Repeat. So simple. So beautiful.

Thank You, Lord, for quiet walks with You
and those seasons of refreshment. Amen. —A.H.

Those Overripe Bananas

Be kind and helpful to one another, tender-hearted
[compassionate, understanding], forgiving one another
[readily and freely], just as God in Christ also forgave you.
EPHESIANS 4:32 AMP

That bunch of bananas in the bowl has seen better days. It's now speck-led with enough nasty brown spots that you are totally grossed out and ready to toss them out. Then you pause to wonder if what lies beneath the peel might still be usable. Perhaps suitable for making a smoothie, or banana nut bread, or even banana pancakes. In fact, you discover that the fruit underneath is so perfectly ripe it's as sweet as candy.

In human terms we tend to judge people like we do that bowl of fruit. What at first glance might appear to be ugly or worthless or something ready to toss may in fact turn out to be the best thing or person you've ever known. Perhaps that woman you dismissed could have been your next business partner or best friend. Or maybe she has the gift of kind-ness, and she was about to offer you the encouragement and support you'd been praying to God for.

Bottom line—best not to judge people. Appearances can be de-ceiving. Each person is made in God's image and useful and unique and glorious in ways we cannot even imagine.

Lord, help me to not judge but to love. Amen. —A.H.

The Ultimate Confidence—Belonging

But you belong to God, my dear children. You have already won a victory over those people, because the Spirit who lives in you is greater than the spirit who lives in the world.

1 JOHN 4:4 NLT

Young people, old people, and everyone in between will try their hardest to find a group, club, gang, organization, or society where they can fit in. A place they feel at home, surrounded by like-minded people who fulfill that basic sense of belonging.

There is another kind of belonging we humans crave—the spiritual kind. An aching of the soul. It is a need we cannot fully explain in human terms, since it transcends mere words and enters into the spiritual realm. Mankind was made in God's image, and we were made for friendship with Him. When we broke off the relationship, it left us with a terrible empty space in our souls—a hollowness in our spirits that only our Lord can fill.

Christ—He alone is the definitive answer to that spiritual void that humankind created long ago. The Lord fulfills that universal desire of belonging, because we belong to Him. And that's the ultimate confidence we will ever find in this life.

Lord Jesus, I accept Your redemptive power, and I ask You to fill that void in my soul with Your love! Amen. —A.H.

Pinched Fingers

*"For I know the plans I have for you," declares the L*ORD*,*
"plans to prosper you and not to harm you,
plans to give you hope and a future."

JEREMIAH 29:11

Your dearest friend has invited you to lunch, and while you're blissfully sipping your tea, she suddenly narrows her eyes at you and says, "I don't at all like what you just said." Then wild-eyed, she proceeds to reach across the table and pinch your fingers with her dainty teaspoon! You would, of course, cry out in pain and then pull back in shock, anger, and confusion. Why? Because the person you loved and trusted zapped you before you even had a chance to explain yourself.

Too many times this is how we perceive God in the way He deals with people. That He is almost eagerly waiting for the moment when He can punish us for one wrong move. Yes, God may indeed discipline us from time to time, but only as any good and loving parent would. The Lord is full of patience and mercy. He loves us and wants the very best for us.

If we know God, truly know His whole nature, then we can have confidence in our comings and goings. Our future. Our everything.

Lord, I'm so grateful that You are a God of mercy and patience
and that You have a marvelous plan for me. Amen. —A.H.

Heart Close

When a mother begins to sing those empty-nest blues, it is a wailing song for sure. Why? Because a mom feels a connection with her child that is sacred and almost mystical. After all, a mother shares her very body with that same child for nine miraculous months. So when your child goes away, you work on ways to keep her heart close. If this is not love, what is?

According to scripture, the Lord feels a similar bond with us. In Old Testament times, God chose to reside in His holy tent—the Tabernacle—to live among and move through the desert with His people. He wanted to be ever near them because of their special heart-connection. If this is not love, then what is?

In New Testament times, we see that Christ came to Earth to be near to us, to live among us, to delight in us, and to save our very souls. If this is not love, then what is?

*Lord, I love the way You love me, and I want to abide
under Your protective wings forever! Amen. —A.H.*

Witnessing with Confidence

Taking the five loaves and the two fish and looking up to heaven, he gave thanks and broke the loaves. Then he gave them to his disciples to distribute to the people. He also divided the two fish among them all. They all ate and were satisfied.

MARK 6:41–42

You're sitting with a stranger at the airport and the subject of religion comes up. You feel a sudden need to bolt. Why? Because you're mortified, not knowing what to say about Christ.

Well then, simply tell her how it goes with you and the Lord. What He means to you personally. And don't forget kindness when she tells you she hates Christians. She might just be checking out how sincere you really are.

And we should never give up on witnessing because we're afraid we don't know enough of the Bible. Yes, studying God's Word is always good. So is taking a class in apologetics, but remember that people are more inclined to embrace Christ after experiencing an honest, winsome, and loving attitude than after hearing an intimidating barrage of biblical facts. Also, it might help to know that God can use our earnest offerings no matter how small, so pray during your chat and then pray afterward, "Holy Spirit, I'm not sure I said the perfect words, but like the loaves and fishes offered with a sincere heart, transform my witness into something usable for Your kingdom."

Lord, show me how to be confident in my witnessing. Amen. —A.H.

What Really Matters

I pray that your love will overflow more and more, and that you will keep on growing in knowledge and understanding. For I want you to understand what really matters, so that you may live pure and blameless lives until the day of Christ's return.

PHILIPPIANS 1:9–10 NLT

It is ridiculously easy to get sidetracked in this life. Everything seems crucial at the time. People are needy—right this minute. Work and to-do lists are piling up. We get caught up in a daily whirlwind of all things urgent. Then, of course, there is all that "other" stuff we don't want anyone to know about. We might spend more time than we'd like to admit social-media browsing, TV binge-watching, techno-gadget twiddling, internet shopping, and. . .well, you get the picture.

We all need good work with godly purpose as well as healthy amounts of restful and refreshing downtime. But when we distill a week to see how our hours really get spent and what was truly accomplished, it might be beneficial to ask, "Did I use my time wisely? Did I make my choices using God's precepts? Did I spend time with the Lord, growing in knowledge and understanding? Did my focus stay on the Lord, and did my heart flow with love for all people?"

Lord, my God, please help me to choose with confidence what is truly important in Your kingdom! Amen. —A.H.

That Last Puzzle Piece

Being confident of this, that he who began a good work in
you will carry it on to completion until the day of Christ Jesus.
PHILIPPIANS 1:6

That puzzle on the dining room table—a little girl in her prettiest blue dress—is coming along nicely. But just as you finish the scene, you realize that there is one piece missing that is supposed to go right smack-dab in the middle. Oy! You shake your fist. Then you try for a mode of acceptance, but no mind games are going to soften the frustration of what could have been. Until that last piece falls into place, the puzzle is no more than an unfinished image—a portrait with a ton of beautiful potential but with something vital missing!

And so it goes with our Lord. We can shake our fists at the heavens or try to make our lives complete on our own, but alas, what we really need to do is embrace our Savior. Christ alone is the most important piece to our life-puzzle. Only He can fill in that gap with His tender mercy, His redemptive power, and His transforming love.

Then, the portrait of that little girl will be made whole—and all that glorious potential will be realized.

Lord, thank You that I can be confident in this. . .that You, who began
a good work in me, will carry it on to completion. Amen. —A.H.

Need Confidence?

Have you not known? Have you not heard?
The LORD is the everlasting God,
the Creator of the ends of the earth.
He does not faint or grow weary;
his understanding is unsearchable.
He gives power to the faint,
and to him who has no might he increases strength.
Even youths shall faint and be weary,
and young men shall fall exhausted;
but they who wait for the LORD shall renew their strength;
they shall mount up with wings like eagles;
they shall run and not be weary;
they shall walk and not faint.
ISAIAH 40:28–31 ESV

After reading this passage in Isaiah, if you still don't have confidence in the God we serve, please read it again. God is mighty, unsearchable, and everlasting. He not only watches over your comings and goings, but He is also powerful enough to change the course of human history—and the course of your life. He alone can make good come out of all the bad that the world throws at you. He is the perfect combination of justice and love, so you don't have to fear that God will be unfaithful and capricious like the world. If you wait on the Lord, He promises to increase your strength.

Yes, we serve a God who is full of power and who is worthy of our praise and confidence! Draw on these truths when you have need.

Lord, when I grow weary of this world, please renew
my strength! In Jesus' name I pray. Amen. —A.H.

Don't Forget to Smile

A cheerful disposition is good for your health;
gloom and doom leave you bone-tired.

PROVERBS 17:22 MSG

Sometimes Christians are so serious about their faith that they forget to smile. But faith in our Lord does not translate into gloom and doom. It means freedom from the oppression of sin, and it means eternal life, so we have good reason for a cheerful disposition. We have the freedom now to smile, to laugh, to share the hope, to expect a miracle, to relish the day, to praise God, to be confident in our joy, to love with abandon.

Don't leave your smiles and chuckles at home. Humor can instantly change a negative, harsh, or dark atmosphere in the room. Obviously not the poking, mean-spirited kind of wit that is used at the expense of others, but the sweet-scented, jovial variety. You can even venture into heavier topics when your heart is smiling. And witnessing in a winsome, cheery way will be much more likely to be welcomed than the heavy-handed, furrowed-brow approach. Try starting the new day with a brighter, lighter touch, and here's to your joy and your good health!

Lord, I know I tend to get too serious about life.
Please help me to look up and smile. To enjoy my walk
with You by my side. In Jesus' name I pray. Amen. —A.H.

The God We Long For

*God's ways are as mysterious as the pathway of the wind and
as the manner in which a human spirit is infused into the
little body of a baby while it is yet in its mother's womb.*

ECCLESIASTES 11:5 TLB

At times God is a mystery. Should that facet of His character frighten us somehow or make us confused or doubtful or less confident in our walk with Him? Not at all. Would we really want to adore and revere a God who is easily understood? Simply put—no. We want a God who possesses vast wonder, profound power, immeasurable beauty, and unfathomable majesty.

That is the God we long for—and that is the God we serve.

Ecclesiastes puts it so perfectly. "God's ways are as mysterious as the pathway of the wind and as the manner in which a human spirit is infused into the little body of a baby while it is yet in its mother's womb."

So feel confident in the midst of God's mystery, and because of it. And also be assured of His infinite love for us—His infinite love for you.

*Creator God, I may not understand all Your ways,
but I know that You love me and care for me always.
I thank You and praise You for who You are! Amen. —A.H.*

Oh, How He Loves You!

"For the Lord your God has arrived to live among you. He is a mighty Savior. He will give you victory. He will rejoice over you with great gladness; he will love you and not accuse you." Is that a joyous choir I hear? No, it is the Lord himself exulting over you in happy song. "I have gathered your wounded and taken away your reproach."

ZEPHANIAH 3:17–18 TLB

When a woman struggles in her marriage, sometimes the gossips may whisper things like, "Oh, she only pretends to love him. She's just playing him along to get what she wants. I heard she was unfaithful. Her commitment to him is hanging by a thread. No wonder their relationship is falling apart!"

When it comes to our spiritual lives and our walk with the Lord, how many times could someone say these whispers about us? But if it's true—amazingly—the Lord loves us still. He not only cares for us, but He rejoices over us and even sings over us. Imagine! In fact, so deep is God's love for us that He does not want us to stay forever stumbling and suffering in our sin; instead, He wants us to know victory and a close relationship with Him that will span all of eternity. Now that's something that every tongue should wag about!

Thank You, Lord, for coming to live among us and for being my Savior and my greatest love! Amen. —A.H.

When the Whole World Laughs

I strain to reach the end of the race and receive the
prize for which God is calling us up to heaven
because of what Christ Jesus did for us.

PHILIPPIANS 3:14 TLB

Do you ever feel like the whole world is laughing at you? That no matter how hard you strain to live a good Christian life, to share the Gospel, and do good deeds, that your efforts seem useless? Maybe you feel like when you cry out at all the injustices of the world, the cruelty, the darkness that gets darker by the day, that you are being drowned out by a relentless blare of evil.

How can we win? How can we press on under these conditions? How can we be encouraged? Take heart. The war has already been won—through Christ's sacrifice on the cross and through His resurrection. May we all remember this truth in every unbearable week, every impossible day, and every breath we take. And may we embrace the promise that God will someday summon us home to heaven. So even if we feel the whole world is laughing at us for our faith, may we ever stay focused on the path that the Lord has set before us and on the glorious prize to come!

Lord God, may I remain confident in You and faithful
in my daily walk. In Jesus' name I pray. Amen. —AH.

Priceless!

*Giving thanks to the Father, who has qualified us to share
in the inheritance of the saints (God's people) in the Light.*
COLOSSIANS 1:12 AMP

Okay, so you find an old ring in a dusty corner of the attic and you think, *Hmm. I wonder if it could be worth anything.* Before long your imagination takes off, and then you declare, "Maybe the stones are precious and it's worth a fortune. Yes!"

So with your excitement building by the minute, you take it into a jewelry store for an appraisal. After the expert does her thing, she shrugs and says, "It's worth about twenty-five bucks." Your heart sighs and your shoulders sag as you hear your mouth reply, "That's all it's worth? Really?"

Thank God that our inheritance through Christ is not only real, but it's priceless. Our redemption and our eternal life are precious gifts that should never be misplaced in the attic of our lives, but treasures that should be celebrated daily!

Is your excitement building? It should be. Someday as you enter the gates of heaven, there will be no hearts sighing or shoulders sagging from sadness or disappointment. The best Earth day imaginable will not come close to the glory of stepping into the light and love and joy of heaven!

*Oh Lord, thank You for Your rich inheritance and
for welcoming me into Your kingdom! Amen. —A.H.*

Fear Not

So do not fear, for I am with you; do not be dismayed,
for I am your God. I will strengthen you and help you;
I will uphold you with my righteous right hand.

ISAIAH 41:10

What would you say is your biggest opponent of confidence? Most women can give plenty of examples: "I hate it when I feel like I don't fit in." Or, "There's nothing worse than walking into a room and not really knowing anyone. I wish I could be invisible." And one more: "There's a woman at work who makes me feel like we're in competition with each other. Just being around her drains me of my confidence."

Behind every scenario that cuts into our confidence is the common denominator of fear. Look again at those examples, and recognize that ensnaring fear that erodes confidence: the fear of what people will think of us.

Yet God often gives the loving directive in His Word to "Fear not!" or, in more modern translations, "Don't be afraid!" When fear has us focus on what others will think, then our focus is actually on ourselves. When we give our fears to God and keep our eyes on Him, then we are free to turn our attention to others with loving care.

Dear God, please replace my fears with faith and renewed
confidence in You. Help me to look always to You so
I can focus on others and their needs. Amen. —J.M.

God, Our Rock

The L<small>ORD</small> is my rock, my fortress and my deliverer;
my God is my rock, in whom I take refuge, my shield
and the horn of my salvation, my stronghold.
P<small>SALM</small> 18:2

Almost sixty times in scripture God is described as our rock. What does that mean to you? Does an image perhaps come to mind of a large rock where you live?

For an online adventure, search the internet for "the world's largest rocks." The results will lead you to photos of familiar monoliths like El Capitan in California's Yosemite National Park or the Rock of Gibraltar in Spain. Others may be less familiar, like the Zuma Rock in the capital of Nigeria. All are impressive!

Bible scholars tell us that the metaphor of God as our rock refers to His constancy, strength, and power. What a contrast to the fickleness and weakness of us humans! God as our rock offers a sure foundation on which to build our lives and families. You probably recall the old Sunday school song still sung today about the foolish man building his house on the sand and the wise man building his on the rock.

What is your foundation today, the crumbling facades of this world or God our rock? When we know God is our rock—our strong, constant foundation—then we can face anything in our lives with confidence.

Lord, thank You for being our solid rock
in this ever-changing world. Amen. —J.M.

What Fills You?

And to know this love that surpasses knowledge—that you
may be filled to the measure of all the fullness of God.

Ephesians 3:19

You may have heard the illustration given of two different kinds of women, demonstrated by how they enter the room of a party. One swoops in with a persona that declares, "Here I am!" while the entrance of the other sings out, "There you are!" The contrast is obvious; the first woman is me-centered, while the second is other-centered.

Let's think about more attributes of the other-centered woman. Her face lights up when she sees you. She is eager to know how *you* are doing instead of launching into everything related to her. Even when she answers her phone, you hear the welcome in her voice.

The other-centered woman overflows with what is inside of her—the love of Jesus. Because she knows she is deeply and unconditionally loved by God, she can forget about herself and focus on others. Because she has accepted God's truth about her worth, she embraces others as worthy. Because her security is in Christ, she lives and loves with the freedom that comes from knowing Him.

You may see shades of yourself in both examples, but don't you long to be like the woman whose life is an effervescent fountain of the love of Jesus?

Jesus, we pray to be so filled with You that
only Your love spills out of us. Amen. —J.M.

Perception Is Everything

The woman said to Him, "Sir, I perceive that You are a prophet."
JOHN 4:19 NKJV

"Perception is everything" became a well-known quote for a reason; it is based on truth.

During a library fund-raiser dinner, one table host threw out some well-known titles to generate conversation. Sparks flew in the dynamic dialogue, with opposing opinions: "I hated that book!" was countered by "I loved that book!" Same words read, but the perceptions of the book's content and quality matched chasms as wide as the Grand Canyon.

In another example, an editor of a series of heartfelt stories was surprised by the low ratings of one reviewer—so different from the glowing feedback of others. The editor soon realized the negative evaluations only accompanied stories about motherhood, and she learned, sadly, that the woman had never been able to have children. Stories that tugged on the heartstrings of the other reviewers ripped her heart in two. Again, same words but contrasting perceptions.

The book examples reflect life, don't they? Our perceptions depend on our personal stories, defined by the individual lens of our lives. If others have failed us, we perhaps perceive that people aren't trustworthy. If we've been disappointed, we don't dare to hope. If love isn't returned, we may feel unlovable. Every human misconception also affects our perception of God. Choose His perspectives, and rightly perceive—and enjoy!—His measureless love for you.

Lord, help my perceptions to always
be based on Your truth. Amen. —J.M.

Knowing Our God

*I keep asking that the God of our Lord Jesus Christ,
the glorious Father, may give you the Spirit of wisdom
and revelation, so that you may know him better.*

Ephesians 1:17

We all heard the warning as kids, "Never trust a stranger." That admonition was given for good reason and still applies in adulthood. We can't trust someone we don't know. We can't know the character of strangers and their motives. And because a stranger doesn't know us, why would we believe that person has our best interest in mind?

That is why it's so important that we intimately *know* our God. Not just know about Him, but that we truly know who He is—the God of love, compassion, and forgiveness. The God who desires a personal relationship with us, who is interested in every detail of our lives. How can we expect to trust God if He's a stranger to us?

We get to know Him by reading His Word and being with Him. Just as we spend time with others to cultivate friendships, it takes time to get to know our Lord and His heart toward us. He loves us! He wants to be with us! As our relationship deepens, we discover that we can trust Him with anything and everything that concerns us. He is no stranger but our loving Friend.

*Thank You, dear Jesus, for the incredible
joy of knowing You. Amen. —J.M.*

Empowered by the Spirit

So he said to me, "This is the word of the Lord
to Zerubbabel: 'Not by might nor by power,
but by my Spirit,' says the Lord Almighty."
ZECHARIAH 4:6

We hear the word *empowerment* a lot in our culture today, especially when it comes to extending it to women. According to Dictionary.com, to empower is to "give power or authority to; authorize, especially by legal or official means." The second meaning is "to enable or permit." So who is the authority deemed worthy enough to empower someone?

And how does empowerment compare to confidence? While it appears empowerment is bestowed, confidence comes from within. As Christian women, God's Spirit dwelling within us is the source of our confidence. We can be assured that our trust in God produces a godly confidence that is pleasing to our Lord.

We don't need to be empowered by human sources when we have the Spirit of God as our guide. He is the One who gives us the boldness to speak and act—not in a harsh or it's-all-about-me way but with a kind and gentle spirit. Nothing can compare to living a life of adventure empowered by the Holy Spirit, while listening to His voice and following His nudges. In Him we have *everything* we need.

Father, thank You that Your Spirit within me provides
all the power and help I need for every day of my life—
from the mundane to the magnificent! Amen. —J.M.

Godfidence

*"But blessed is the one who trusts in the LORD,
whose confidence is in him."*

JEREMIAH 17:7

For those of us who enjoy a vital relationship with Jesus, we have learned that He is our source for everything, including a strong sense of confidence. While our confidence in ourselves can vary as much as the weather, our confidence in God is founded on all His unchangeable and eternal qualities.

In fact, many Christians have come to refer to the confidence that comes from God as *Godfidence*. That term has been around for some time now, and it's even emblazoned on T-shirts, with phrases like "Absolute Trust" following the word. The top definition for Godfidence from the Urban Dictionary is "knowing God is in control."

Godfidence can also be defined as the awareness of God's power and our reliance on God's promises. The confidence God gives equips you with courage to be the person He's made you to be and to do what He's called you to do. Godfidence comes from our God above so that we can live by this truth here on earth: I can't, but God can. It's the difference between knowing we are God-made and not self-made, where we gladly trade a prideful "I've got this!" to a grateful "God's got this!"

*Father, keep us humbly aware that everything we have comes
from Your good hand. Instill in us godly confidence and courage
that will point others to the source: You. Amen. —J.M.*

Encourage One Another

*Therefore encourage one another and build
each other up, just as in fact you are doing.*

1 THESSALONIANS 5:11

In today's world of social media, the realm of relationships often reeks with comparisons and competition instead of camaraderie and community. Picture-perfect photos of kids and homes and meals cause us to squirm with insecurity. Videos of those slimmer, prettier, and funnier make us want to burrow our bodies under our bedcovers; we know we can never match up.

What we tend to forget is that behind every flawless presentation is a reality as real as our own. Just beyond the picturesque Instagram post are piles of unfolded laundry cascading down a couch. Often behind the Facebook photo of the radiant couple is the scene in their pastor's office where they are seeking marriage counseling. And those darling children? They've been known to make their moms yell and cry in frustration too.

We are all imperfect people doing the best we can. That's why the scripture above is important to remember. We need encouragement from one another. Some translations use the words *comfort* and *support* in place of *encourage*. So let's reach beyond phony photos (no pun intended!) and seek to build community as we do this life together with God's help.

*Lord, we need You and we need one another. Help us to discern the
struggles hiding behind the smiles and to strengthen one another
with the encouragement found in You and Your Word. Amen. —J.M.*

Our Words Matter

*May these words of my mouth and this meditation of my heart
be pleasing in your sight, L*ORD*, my Rock and my Redeemer.*

PSALM 19:14

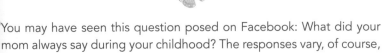

You may have seen this question posed on Facebook: What did your mom always say during your childhood? The responses vary, of course, but many are pretty universal:

> "What part of *no* don't you understand?"
> "Someday your face will freeze like that."
> "Money doesn't grow on trees."
> "No one said life is fair."
> "Eat your vegetables."

The most-repeated words are the ones most remembered. If your family members and friends were polled, what would they list as your choice expressions? Would you identify those phrases as uplifting or downers? Would it please you to be remembered for those words after you are gone?

Let's think about the choice we have every day to determine what comes out of our mouths. Consider saying Bible verses aloud when faced with a challenging time or giving praise to God in our joy of an answered prayer. Or sing hymns in the midst of a hopeless situation. Whatever comprises our daily circumstances, words matter. The ones we say most often can color the lives of those around us with hope or despair. What wise words can we say now that will speak for generations to come?

*Lord, what a gift You gave us in words! May the words we speak
be pleasing to You and a loving legacy to others. Amen. —J.M.*

Mindful Listening and Thinking

Finally, brothers and sisters, whatever is true, whatever is noble, whatever is right, whatever is pure, whatever is lovely, whatever is admirable—if anything is excellent or praiseworthy—think about such things.

PHILIPPIANS 4:8

What we say matters, but what we listen to also matters. Think about what may infiltrate your mind every day: television, gossip, radio talk shows and music, your own negative self-talk, lies from Satan. Everything we hear influences our thoughts, and those thoughts play a major role in our lives.

A woman was working cheerily around her home when she felt her spirits plummet as if a switch had been flipped. She stopped what she was doing, perplexed as to why her upbeat day had just taken a plunge. When she recounted her last thoughts, she realized they had turned to an unresolved, troubling situation with a friend. She was stunned how those thoughts had ushered in gloom like gray clouds bringing in a sudden storm.

Everything we hear, no matter the source, will affect us in a negative or positive way. That mind-set will then influence other elements, including our emotions and even our relationship with Christ. Let's be Philippians 4:8 women, shall we?

Lord, it's easy to be nonchalant and even careless about what enters our minds and hearts. Help us to please You with choices that will benefit us and our walk with You. Amen. —J.M.

Eye the Best, Forget the Rest

Turn my eyes away from worthless things;
preserve my life according to your word.
PSALM 119:37

Are you a visual learner? Do images stick in your mind? Never before has there been so much to see unless one lives as a hermit. Screens surround us with every imaginable scene available with only a click or a swipe. Some women try to be especially careful not to view violent or disturbing images in any form, since they don't want them showing up again as nightmares.

Visuals can sear themselves on the viewer's brain, etched for all time. If it's an inspiring Bible verse, quote, or scene of beauty, then that can be a good thing. But too often the images thrown in front of us could rival "the vile images" that the Israelites had "set [their] eyes on" (Ezekiel 20:7). The instructions given back then? "Get rid" of them!

To be godly women whose faith and confidence are solely settled in God, we need to prayerfully determine what we look at, what we set before our eyes. Perhaps a good test would be to ask ourselves if we'd be comfortable with Jesus sitting beside us on the couch, viewing the same images. After all, He *is* there.

Lord, help us to make wise choices regarding what our
eyes see. May we be mindful and not mindless
as we seek to please You. Amen. —J.M.

Beauty Inside and Out

Your beauty should not come from outward adornment, such as elaborate hairstyles and the wearing of gold jewelry or fine clothes. Rather, it should be that of your inner self, the unfading beauty of a gentle and quiet spirit, which is of great worth in God's sight.
1 PETER 3:3–4

Years ago a woman attended a Christian-based personal improvement course. The lovely, dynamic instructor focused on subjects such as conversation, table manners, and attire. One evening she stated emphatically, "Women feel like they look." She elaborated how important it was to spend time each day on grooming and gave convincing examples of how that practice affects a woman's mind-set and mood.

Think about how you feel when dressed in an attractive outfit, your hair shining, your makeup dewy. Compare that to when you wear sloppy clothing, hide your greasy hair under a baseball cap, and barely manage to brush your teeth. Now reflect on how those opposite images affect your outlook for the day.

Of course, if our hearts are filled with bitterness and resentment, no amount of outer efforts will disguise a sick soul. Over a century ago, a Quaker lady with a beautiful complexion was asked what kind of cosmetics she used. She replied, "I use for my lips, *truth*; for my voice, *prayer*; for my eyes, *pity*; for my hands, *charity*; for my figure, *uprightness*; for my heart, *love*."

Lord, help us to adorn ourselves in such a way that Your beauty shines through. Amen. —J.M.

The Reflection of Radiance

Those who look to him are radiant;
their faces are never covered with shame.
PSALM 34:5

Julie hadn't seen her friend, Rachel, for months, and she was happily stunned by the difference in her countenance. The hardness of her divorced years had melted away, replaced by the glow of joy. Peace and contentment rested on Rachel's face, turning back time with a soft youthfulness. What had made such a difference? Julie soon found out Rachel's face reflected the love from her soon-to-be husband.

Our countenances reveal much about the state of our souls. The shock of sudden grief can alter a face with dark shadows of sadness. Holding a newborn baby can transform a mother's face with beauty that could never come from cosmetics. A fit of anger can disfigure a pleasant face into one that terrifies. What face of yours is most familiar to others?

Also, are you an observer of the countenances you encounter every day? Do you see the looks of despair? Do you see the downcast soul on the dejected face? For those of us who look to Jesus, His joy shines on our faces. The radiance comes because of God's gifts to us: forgiveness, freedom, and the deepest love known to humanity—a love willing to die for us.

Thank You, dear Lord, for shining Your love on us. May the radiance
You give us reach others with Your hope and joy. Amen. —J.M.

Better Together

"I am the vine; you are the branches. If you remain in me and I in you, you will bear much fruit; apart from me you can do nothing."

JOHN 15:5

According to this verse, apart from Jesus, we can do nothing. Does your heart balk at that statement? Do you find it offensive? Are you even now checking off your mental list of abilities that you can perform?

You may be tempted to point to your education, training, and experience to prove your skills. Maybe you have organized functions that display your myriad talents. Perhaps running your home efficiently is your personal fortress of pride.

Ah, there's the stickler: pride. If we look at our accomplishments as being just that—our own—we fail to give God the glory. After all, who provides our next breath? Who gave us our minds for His creative purposes? Who provides the strength for our every accomplishment?

When we depend on Jesus for everything, then we can be confident that the results will bring honor to Him and not to us. His strength and beauty will shine in us because we are connected to the Source of all life. A song of praise will replace a sense of pridefulness.

Jesus, there's no greater privilege and joy than to be connected to You, the life-giving Vine. Help us to always remain in You and bear much fruit for Your kingdom. Amen. —J.M.

Competence: A Gift from God

You show that you are a letter from Christ, the result of our ministry, written not with ink but with the Spirit of the living God, not on tablets of stone but on tablets of human hearts. Such confidence we have through Christ before God. Not that we are competent in ourselves to claim anything for ourselves, but our competence comes from God.

2 CORINTHIANS 3:3–5

The friendship was an unlikely one. She had just moved back to her hometown after being away for a few years. He was a computer tech for a local bank—about the same age as her oldest son—who freelanced on the side.

During conversations while getting her new computer set up, she discovered how bright he was and also how he struggled with anything to do with faith in Jesus. Yet when she was open about her faith, he was receptive. He resisted in one area, however. When he would praise her for something, her first response was to give credit to God. That frustrated her computer-savvy friend, and he told her so. "You need to take some credit!"

Yet she knew the Source of every gift and talent. She knew any competence came from God. She had seen Him provide for her in every realm of her life, and she couldn't help but point others to Him.

*Thank You, dear God, for Your care in
the competence You give us. Amen. —J.M.*

Be with Jesus

*Now when they saw the boldness of Peter and John,
and perceived that they were uneducated and untrained men,
they marveled. And they realized that they had been with Jesus.*

ACTS 4:13 NKJV

What would make others realize we had been with Jesus? Perhaps the kind tone in our voice? An attractive boldness in sharing our faith? Our caring listening when we lean in and give our full attention to what's being said?

When we begin each day with Jesus, we'll "taste and see that the LORD is good" (Psalm 34:8) while reading His Word. We'll discover that "in [His] presence is fullness of joy" (Psalm 16:11 AMP) and be strengthened for the day ahead. In those moments of quietude, we can confide in Him our deepest secrets and desires, and He will whisper His love and wisdom to our waiting hearts.

The demands of life will always vie for your attention, but you will fulfill each one better when you've first spent time with your loving Lord. Make choices that will be life-changing in the best of ways. Get up a few minutes early. Keep off every screen and distraction. Bask in the warmth of His calming presence, and see the difference He makes in your day. Others will notice too. They'll see that you've been with Jesus.

*What a privilege and joy it is to begin our day with You, Jesus.
Thank You for the difference You make daily. Amen. —J.M.*

Be Still

Renee knelt for her morning prayer time, her thoughts teeming with concerns about her family and the day's hectic schedule. The wire of her mental list kept winding tighter around her mind. She had been on her knees several minutes when she realized she hadn't even begun to pray; her thoughts had been running like a hamster spinning in its noisy metal wheel.

She took a deep breath and began singing the words "Be still, and know that I am God," and when God began to speak to her, she penned the words that came:

"Be still in the midst of chaos, and know My care.

Be still in the midst of the hospital room, and know My comfort.

Be still when worry pounds you like the never-ending waves of the sea, and know My peace.

Be still when the noise of life wants to drown out My voice, and know that My words remain true: I will never leave you nor forsake you.

Be still and simply bask in My presence, and know My deep, deep love for you.

Be still.

Know that I am God.

In Me all is well."

Thank You for the stillness found only in You,
Lord, in the hush of Your heart. Amen. —J.M.

God Is Love

And so we know and rely on the love God has for us. God is love.
Whoever lives in love lives in God, and God in them.

1 JOHN 4:16

If you grew up attending church, you probably heard the words *God is love* many times. Sometimes familiarity causes something amazing to lose its luster. So let's park on those three little words and even learn to live there.

God is love. Not God is *like* love. Not God *resembles* love. Not God is a *representation* of love. No. God *is* love. Let those three words of truth go deep inside of you, and allow yourself time to make that truth personal. If God is love, then everything He does flows out of who He is: Love.

Those words can be hard to hear when you're in the midst of a horrible tragedy or grief. Yet over the centuries, in the worst of circumstances, God has shown the timeless and transforming truth of His love. He works in our lives out of His love for us. While we often can't see that truth in the midst of heartbreaking times, we can cling to the One who is love itself and trust Him to hold us close.

Father, my God who is love, thank You for loving me
with a perfect love that never changes. Amen. —J.M.

Christic Living in Us

*"I have been crucified with Christ and I no longer live,
but Christ lives in me. The life I now live in the body, I live by
faith in the Son of God, who loved me and gave himself for me."*

GALATIANS 2:20

Can you echo the apostle Paul's words that you have been "crucified with Christ"? Does the image of being crucified with our Lord make you cringe—or at least squirm? When we think of our Lord's agonizing death on the cross, any "persecution" we may suffer pales next to His, doesn't it?

But here's the beauty of being "crucified with Christ." Everything selfish dies. Think of all the words and ways of living that focus on self: self-centered, self-absorbed, self-promoting, self-confident—and the list goes on. Even self-deprecation and self-consciousness draw attention to one's self.

When we no longer live for ourselves, then Christ can live fully in us. Think on that! Because Christ lives in us, then He can love that difficult family member or friend for us. When He lives in us, then His joy shines, and we don't have to muster up gladness on our own. And when Christ lives in us, then any confidence we possess is the direct result from His constant presence in our lives.

*How amazing it is, our dear Lord, that You live in us!
Every deficit of ours is compensated by Your
divine presence. Praise You! Amen. —J.M.*

No Condemnation

Therefore, there is now no condemnation for those who are in Christ Jesus, because through Christ Jesus the law of the Spirit who gives life has set you free from the law of sin and death.

ROMANS 8:1–2

The word *condemnation* is a mouthful, isn't it, and while the term may not be heard much in everyday conversation, its practice is prevalent in our society. Just read the comments following any online news story. The caustic words condemning the actions of the people involved could curl anyone's toes. When you add the hostile bickering between the ones making the comments, enough sparks fly to start a blazing fire.

Synonyms for condemnation expand the reasons we like to avoid coming under its curse: accusation, censure, denouncement, reproach, disapproval, judgment, and blame. The weight of those words causes us to welcome the relief of the antonyms: approval, compliment, endorsement, praise, acquittal, freeing, and pardon.

Read the verse again at the top of this page, and savor its truth. That little word *no* makes all the difference, doesn't it? Because Christ Jesus pardoned us by His death and resurrection, we are no longer condemned. We are free. Instead of living under the heavy blanket of condemnation, we live by the Spirit who gives life.

Thank You, Jesus, that because we are in You we can live in confidence and not under condemnation. Help us to walk in that freeing truth today. Amen. —J.M.

Be Bold!

Therefore, since we have a great high priest who has ascended into heaven, Jesus the Son of God, let us hold firmly to the faith we profess. For we do not have a high priest who is unable to empathize with our weaknesses, but we have one who has been tempted in every way, just as we are—yet he did not sin. Let us then approach God's throne of grace with confidence, so that we may receive mercy and find grace to help us in our time of need.
HEBREWS 4:14–16

What is your "time of need" right now? What answer from God are you most seeking? What is it that is most troubling you today? A crumbling relationship? A recent medical diagnosis? A prodigal child? A devastating loss? Fear of the future?

Today's scripture is laden with encouragement. Since Jesus is our high priest, we have reason to hold firmly to our faith. He empathizes with our struggles. And we can go to God's throne of grace not with timidity or fear but with confidence—or boldness, according to some translations. When we do, we will receive His loving mercy and grace for whatever hard thing we are facing.

So when troubles overwhelm, don't go immediately to your phone. Talking about a problem will often enlarge it. Instead, let's go first to the throne of the One who will provide exactly what we need.

God, we come to You in confidence today,
asking for Your help. Amen. —J.M.

Our Perfect Confidence

For the LORD will be your confidence,
And will keep your foot from being caught.
PROVERBS 3:26 NKJV

We continue to come back to the truth that God desires all of us to capture: He is our confidence. We don't have to conjure up confidence on our own or seek it elsewhere. Every other thing and person on this planet will fail us and come up lacking, but God, the perfect One, is our perfect confidence.

Maybe even now you recall times when others have failed or betrayed you. The mental list may leave a bitter taste in your mouth, and you recoil from the thought of trusting anyone again. You'd rather wrap yourself in a cocoon of protection than allow your heart to be hurt again.

Too often we transfer that attitude to God, forgetting that He cannot fail us. When we look to Him to be our confidence, then we will have the courage to do whatever He leads us to do: to forgive and ask for forgiveness, to love the unlovable, to dare to trust again.

To act in obedience "will keep your foot from being caught" and taking a tumble into the barren lands of bitterness and self-protection. Because God is our confidence, we can live this life with a serenity that can only be described as divine.

Lord, we thank You for being our confidence
and that we can completely depend on You
for every situation we encounter. Amen. —J.M.

This Same Jesus

Jesus Christ is the same yesterday and today and forever.
HEBREWS 13:8

What in your life has remained absolutely the same over the years? Consider where you've lived. How about your relationship with family and friends? Think about your job situation.

You get the point. Even if you're one of the rare ones to live in the same house all your life or work at one job, changes occur within those realms, such as a remodel or reclassification. The undeniable truth is we live in a world of constant change. With the added aspect of instant news and social media, we are now more aware of those changes than ever before.

Today's verse in Hebrews offers a contrast so vast that we can scarcely comprehend it. Jesus is the same? He doesn't change a whit? His love and grace never diminish when we fail Him once again? Yes, no, and no! We are tempted to think of our Lord in human terms, making Him as fickle as fans of a football team—loyal when their team is winning and jeering when their team is losing.

The opposite of the word *same* reveals what Jesus isn't: changing and inconsistent, wavering and variable. He loves us constantly and consistently. No. Matter. What.

*Jesus, we can't begin to comprehend the constancy of
Your love, but we are so grateful for that indelible truth.
Thank You for Your inability to change. Amen. —J.M.*

Believing the Impossible

"Blessed is she who believed, for there will be a fulfillment
of those things which were told her from the Lord."
LUKE 1:45 NKJV

When the angel Gabriel appeared to Mary as recorded in Luke 1, their brief conversation was not only life-changing for the entire world but also, of course, for Mary. We can't help but admire how she moved from being "troubled" (Luke 1:29) by his greeting of "highly favored" (Luke 1:28) to receiving his succinct words regarding the child she would be carrying.

After she heard Gabriel's startling news, she simply asked, "How will this be, since I am a virgin?" The angel explained how it would be by "the power of the Most High" (Luke 1:35), but he didn't stop there. He went on to tell her how her relative Elizabeth, the one "who was called barren" (Luke 1:36 NKJV), had conceived a son in her old age.

Then Gabriel gave the wrap-up of his three-pronged pronouncement: "For with God nothing will be impossible" (Luke 1:37 NKJV).

Haven't we all had those moments when we've asked God, "How can this be?" after we've been given a promise from Him? What follows those first four words is the word *since*. How would you finish that question to God regarding His promise to you? Fill in the blank: "How can this be, since _____?"

Then remember His timeless truth: "For with God nothing will be impossible."

Lord, we believe You for the impossible. Amen. —J.M.

Stillness for the Storm

The disciples went and woke him, saying, "Master, Master,
we're going to drown!" He got up and rebuked the wind
and the raging waters; the storm subsided, and all was calm.

LUKE 8:24

While little is known about the author of the hymn "Be Still, My Soul," the lyrics suggest that Katharina von Schlegel suffered sorrows and difficulties. The era in which she lived in Germany, 1697 to 1768, surely contributed to life's perils. Writers have speculated that she experienced a "shaking" in her faith but emerged even stronger as seen in the second verse:

> "Be still, my soul: thy God doth undertake
> To guide the future as He has the past.
> Thy hope, thy confidence, let nothing shake;
> All now mysterious shall be bright at last.
> Be still, my soul: the waves and winds still know
> His voice who ruled them while He dwelt below."

Is something shaking your confidence these days? A medical diagnosis? The sudden loss of a loved one? The devastating ending of a relationship? Perhaps it's the uncertainty of living in times that feel as unstable as shifting sand and as turbulent as stormy waves of the sea. Or maybe you just feel adrift, uncertain as to God's plans and purposes for your life.

Take heart in God, the calmer of storms. "Will Your Anchor Hold?" is another hymn that reminds us, "We have an anchor that keeps the soul steadfast and sure while the billows roll."

Lord, please still my soul, and fill me with Your peace. Amen. —J.M.

A Heart That Sings

*My heart, O God, is steadfast, my heart
is steadfast; I will sing and make music.*

PSALM 57:7

The verse from Psalm 57 portrays David with a steadfast heart and
singing to God. His declaration makes us think that life was going well
for him, right? But, in truth, David had just escaped from Saul and was
living in a cave.

The first six verses of the psalm paint a different picture of the
state of his heart when he implores, "Have mercy on me, my God,
have mercy on me" and "I cry out to God Most High." Other phrases
give us visuals of his despair: "I am in the midst of lions" and "I was
bowed down in distress."

Can you relate to David's heart cries to God and his fearsome difficulties? What are the lions in your life? Let's look at one sentence that
is layered in the middle of his laments: "God sends forth his love and
his faithfulness." It's as if David decided to remind himself of that truth
before he launched into the subject of lions.

And then by verse seven his heart lands in a doubly steadfast place.
Other translations for *steadfast* enhance the meaning: confident, un-
wavering, fixed, committed, secure, determined. David sought God for
mercy, found him faithful, and then he decided to sing.

Shall we join him?

*Lord, no matter what cave of captivity we are in today, may we seek
Your mercy, find You faithful, and sing Your praises. Amen.* —J.M.

Life Overflowing

*The thief does not come except to steal, and to kill,
and to destroy. I have come that they may have life,
and that they may have it more abundantly.*
JOHN 10:10 NKJV

Don't we love the promise of an abundant life? Yet what exactly does that look like? The dictionary definitions of *abundant*—richly supplied, oversufficient, abounding—line up with the meanings given in other translations of the Bible: "in its fullest measure," "more plenteously," "till it overflows."

Jesus came to give us life—His life within us—so that our lives will naturally overflow out of His abundance. But does that abundance include only good things? Or is it a fullness of all things that life has to offer?

A fullness of life isn't made up of only picnics and ice-cream parties. A diet of everything good and happy, with no challenges, would make us fat and flabby in our character. Instead, God knows to provide an array of offerings for our lives that will show who He is within us. The apostle Paul exemplified a life of fullness, with everything from prison stays to shipwrecks, and his writings are filled with an infectious joy.

God wired us to thrive in even the fullness of overflowing laundry baskets, endless choices how to spend our time, and countless problems that need resolving. He replaces a former life of emptiness with His fullness.

*We are grateful, God, for the abundant
life found in You. Amen. —J.M.*

More or Less

So don't be afraid; you are worth more than many sparrows.
MATTHEW 10:31

A boy's aunt spoke unthinkable words to him, the middle child: "Why can't you be as smart as your sister or as good looking as your brother?" Decades later, when that boy-now-pastor relayed those words, it was obvious they had been etched into his memory forever by the stylus of pain. He felt "less than."

When have you felt "less than"? When have you felt you can't measure up to those around you? We've all been there at some point in our lives due to a careless comment, a less-than-stellar performance on our part, or even because of facial expressions or body language from others that silently announce our unworthiness—our "less than."

The phrase *less than* comes up only eight times on Bible Gateway in the New International Version. But, the words *more than* appear 205 times. While the context varies widely, that informal survey is an indicator of our God's heart. Because of Him, we are more than we could ever be without Him.

The next time you feel "less than," look to our Father God, who deems you to be "more than" you could ever dream.

Jesus, may I hear and see only the truth of Your "more than"
when I'm tempted to believe the lie of "less than." Amen. —J.M.

Wise Choices

Our daily choices determine the direction of our lives:

Choose to worry or to trust God.
Choose the ways of the world or choose the Way, Jesus, our Savior.
Choose the paralysis of fear or choose the freedom of faith.
Choose to run ahead of God or choose to follow Him.
Choose to spend time in His life-giving Word or choose to look at life-draining words.
Choose to dabble in the things of darkness or choose to live in the Light of the World.
Choose the empty, temporal lies of the devil or choose the rich, eternal truth of Jesus.

These are choices that leave no room for middle ground, no room for compromise. Either you choose to live in God's camp, or you choose to wander in the wilderness of the world. In God's camp you'll know His shelter and sustenance and support. In the wilderness you'll find desolation and darkness and despair.

Where you choose to dwell will determine the quality of your life and the measure of your contentment. Even the small decisions of each day indicate the direction of our hearts. Choose wisely, and enjoy the benefits of your choices—both now and into eternity.

Lord, we desire to choose You in our every decision.
Help us stay close to You, with our hearts attuned to
Your voice of wisdom and guidance. Amen. —J.M.

Getting Through

But the Israelites went through the sea on dry ground,
with a wall of water on their right and on their left.
Exodus 14:29

After getting through every daunting project with a deadline, a busy mom and writer is known for saying, "I'm so glad to be to this point!" In fact, she teases her family about putting those words on her grave marker someday.

What difficulties have you come through? Perhaps it was a grueling treatment for illness, a major move, or getting through the darkest days of grief after a heartbreaking loss. We can offer a collective sigh of relief when together we recall our times of "getting through."

But what about now? What about the situation that seems forever, when you feel stuck in a quagmire of questions? The woman still waiting to be a bride or mother. The entrepreneur whose dreams are constricted by a lack of finances. The mom with a prodigal. The weary caregiver in a longtime commitment.

Look to our fellow travelers in the Bible. God brought the children of Israel *through* the Red Sea and the desert. God brought Joseph *through* his years of betrayal and imprisonment. God didn't leave Jonah in the cavern of the large fish, nor will He leave you in the circumstances now constraining you. Whether He provides here or on the highway to heaven, you can be confident our faithful God will carry you *through*.

Lord, thank You that dead-end streets
don't exist in kingdom living. Amen. —J.M.

Our Father's Eyes

For the eyes of the Lord run to and fro throughout the whole earth, to show Himself strong on behalf of those whose heart is loyal to Him.

2 Chronicles 16:9 nkjv

The human eye is one of God's many miracles, the second most complex organ after the brain. The human eye contains more than two million operational parts that process up to 35,000 bits of information every hour. Amazing! A fingerprint has 40 unique characteristics, but an iris has 256. Out of all the muscles in your body, the muscles that control your eye are the most active.

The Bible talks about eyes in a variety of contexts. Jesus not only healed blind eyes, but God also opened the eyes of Balaam and Elisha's servant so they could see beyond the physical and into the spiritual realm. Many accounts tell of those who found favor in God's eyes, like Noah.

The majority of the five hundred verses about eyes focus on the eyes of people. But let's consider the eyes of God as mentioned in the scripture above. He sees us and longs to "show Himself strong" to those loyal to him. Psalm 34:15 (niv) tells us, "The eyes of the Lord are on the righteous, and his ears are attentive to their cry." God's eyes on us shine with His love for us.

Thank You, Father, for looking on us with Your loving care.
Help us to keep our eyes only on You. Amen. —J.M.

Keeping Our Distance

But Peter followed him at a distance, right up to the courtyard of the high priest. He entered and sat down with the guards to see the outcome.

MATTHEW 26:58

Picture an owner training her dog to heel and seeing the dog behind her, sniffing in some bushes, paying no heed to its master. Now see a small child trailing well behind his mom, ignoring her pleas to come closer. And then see Peter, following our Lord "at a distance" after Jesus had been arrested in the Garden of Gethsemane.

We may be tempted to say that we wouldn't have been like Peter. We'd like to think that we would have remained by Jesus with steadfast loyalty during his time of utmost testing. Earlier we're told, "Then all the disciples deserted him and fled" (v. 56). Yes, Peter followed "at a distance," but at least he showed up, in spite of his three vehement denials of even knowing Jesus.

Are we following Jesus at a distance? Allowing for space between Him and us so that we can turn and flee like the disciples? Perhaps God gave us the perfect opportunity to talk about Him, but we chose silence instead. Or God nudged us to pray for someone right then and there, but we didn't want to draw any attention to ourselves in a public place. When we don't follow His leadings, we put "distance" between Jesus and us.

Jesus, we pray to stay near You. Amen. —J.M.

Who Are You?

Simon Peter, a servant and apostle of Jesus Christ,
To those who through the righteousness of our God and
Savior Jesus Christ have received a faith as precious as ours.

2 PETER 1:1

What labels do you wear? No, not the labeled tags in your clothing giving the brand name of the maker. What "labels" apply to you? How do you desire to be known? Think of the descriptors on your Facebook page or on your Instagram and Twitter accounts. If social media isn't your thing, what do you tell someone when asked about yourself?

If a list of labels were compiled from the readers of this book, it would undoubtedly be vast, with many overlapping. See how many of these terms apply to you: wife, mom, homeschooling parent, coffee or tea drinker, chocolate lover, domestic goddess (or domestic arts nerd!), creative, music addict, Sunday school teacher, foodie, walker.

Yet what do you want to be known for the most? Many Christian women depict themselves online as a "follower of Jesus" with various qualifiers: a girl following hard after Jesus, grateful follower of Jesus, imperfect follower of Jesus. In doing so, they align themselves with Peter, James, Paul, and other New Testament writers who saw themselves as "a servant. . .of Jesus Christ."

Lord, we pray not only to be defined like Your
disciples—servants of Jesus Christ—but also to
live that way in humble obedience. Amen. —J.M.

Learning from Jesus

"Come to me, all you who are weary and burdened, and I will give you rest. Take my yoke upon you and learn from me, for I am gentle and humble in heart, and you will find rest for your souls. For my yoke is easy and my burden is light."

MATTHEW 11:28–30

Jesus gave us the perfect example of a confident person when he walked this earth. His confidence was based in His Father and was permeated with humility—the perfect combination. His God-given confidence upturned tables, drove the money changers from the temple, and also led Him on the path to Calvary.

When confidence is manufactured from within, then pride tends to creep in, turning confidence into arrogance. Even humility isn't immune to pride when it becomes self-effacing and false. Self-generated qualities always exalt self. The cure is to seek God as our source and to glorify Him.

You are probably familiar with the above passage of scripture and maybe memorized it as a child. But read it again, and this time linger on the words "learn from me, for I am gentle and humble in heart." Let's learn from our Lord, shall we? The gentle and humble heart of Jesus is our pattern to follow, our ideal to emulate.

Jesus, what an honor and privilege it is to learn from You. Thank You for Your beautiful example of confidence that shines with humility. We love You. Amen. —J.M.

Blessed Are You

"Blessed are those who are persecuted because of righteousness,
for theirs is the kingdom of heaven. Blessed are you when
people insult you, persecute you and falsely say all kinds
of evil against you because of me."
MATTHEW 5:10–11

We can't truly appreciate having trust and confidence in Jesus unless we acquaint ourselves with today's persecuted Church. Biographies from the past tell of these faithful saints, but with the internet we can now know what is going on worldwide with our brothers and sisters in Christ. The accounts both convict and sober us when we hear of their sufferings—and their amazing faith.

Muslims are turning to Jesus daily in record numbers, often after He has appeared to them in a dream or vision. They testify to disillusionment with their religion, wearied by rituals and remaining empty inside. Once they meet Jesus and experience the peace and joy only He can give, they are resolute to serve Him no matter what. It isn't uncommon that they lose everything: their families, homes, and jobs—and sometimes their lives.

Yet what matters is that they can't lose the one thing most precious to them—their newfound faith in the One they love the most: Jesus.

Lord, we can't imagine that kind of persecution. Help us to
always stand for You, if only in the face of ridicule. And help us to
remember to pray for Your family around the world. Amen. —J.M.

Real for Real

Make this your common practice: Confess your sins to each other and pray for each other so that you can live together whole and healed.
JAMES 5:16 MSG

While we may admire those who appear to have it all together, they aren't usually the ones we gravitate toward for friendship. The picture of perfection intimidates, while authenticity attracts. The woman who lets you see her reality—piles of unfolded laundry, dishes piled in the sink, crunchy cereal on the kitchen floor—is the woman who allows you to be real.

How many times have we read social media comments about that very scenario? The woman who gives us a peek beyond the staged Instagram photo—showing the mess on the perimeters and laughing about it—garners comments of gratitude for not hiding the clutter. The mom who posts about her regret at yelling at her kids is the mom who reminds us of ourselves, and we heave a sigh of relief.

We all have realms we'd rather hide than display. The woman who knows God loves her unconditionally can enjoy her expertise in organizational skills but also share her painful frustrations in parenting. Like a clear pane of glass, our transparency allows others to see us as we are, and together we can celebrate our successes and encourage one another in our struggles.

Lord, help us to be real and to uplift
others in their reality. Amen. —J.M.

Every Little Thing

Don't worry about anything; instead, pray about everything.
Tell God what you need, and thank him for all he has done.

PHILIPPIANS 4:6 NLT

The ad in the women's magazine boasted these words: "Confidence. Shipped Free." The product? House paint. The accompanying photo showed a dining room decked out in two contrasting shades. If you're like many, you need that confidence shipped beforehand, when you're agonizing over choosing the right paint colors.

From the time we wake up and throw off our bedcovers until the time we climb back into bed that night, we make countless decisions about lots of little things. That process can be exhausting at times—think about an extensive shopping trip with limited funds—since we want to make the right choices. Yet how often do we go to God for His ideas and counsel?

While some scoff at praying over even the smallest of matters, others have seen God's love in His specific guidance. When a young mom felt stymied one evening about what to fix for dinner, she sent up a simple prayer for help. Instantly an idea came to mind that hadn't occurred to her earlier. The resulting good meal garnered exuberant praise from her family that evening and reminded the cook how God cares about the smallest of details.

Lord, Your loving care amazes us. Help us turn to You first to
see what creative guidance You desire to give us. Amen. —J.M.

Savoring the Seasons

There is a time for everything, and a season
for every activity under the heavens.
ECCLESIASTES 3:1

"I wish I'd known how much life there is after children," a mother with grown children confided to a younger mom. "I tried to do it all because I felt I'd be too old to do anything worthwhile after my children left home." With a rueful smile, she shook her head. "Silly me! How wrong and shortsighted I was."

That same mom recounted how she couldn't wait until all the kids were out of diapers and then yearned for when a babysitter would no longer be needed. Those seemingly endless seasons are now a long-ago memory. An even earlier memory remains fixed, when she was pining for her thirteenth birthday, the threshold to finally becoming an official teenager. Her father's wise words then echo even today: "Don't wish your life away."

What season are you living in right now? Whether difficult or easy, lonely or joyful, every season passes. Remember, it's only a season, a season entwined with God's purposes. The secret is to enjoy the season you are in, to be satisfied in it. How do we do that? We can begin by being thankful for babies that need diapers and to hold them close while we can.

Lord, every season has its challenges and joys, and we pray to
embrace and enjoy the season You have us in right now. Amen. —J.M.

Only Jesus Satisfies

When I came to you, I did not come with eloquence or human wisdom as I proclaimed to you the testimony about God.
1 CORINTHIANS 2:1

Krista feels blessed that she grew up in the Church, where she heard lots of stories. Those stories often took the form of testimonies during the informal services of Sunday evening and Wednesday night prayer meeting. Sometimes the stories were told with tears or laughter—or both!—but they always shared a common theme: only Jesus satisfies.

Many testified to lives of misery before Christ and lives of joy after Christ. Krista heard about lifestyles foreign to her and the emptiness that accompanied them. She saw smiles and a glow on faces that indicated God's radiant presence in their lives.

When Krista went off to college and found a freedom she hadn't known before, she took with her a suitcase of stories. A trunkful of testimonies. A wardrobe of God's wonders.

In her new environment, she questioned if she wanted to remain true to her faith in Jesus. The answer came easily. Why should she make the same mistakes and deal with regrets when she didn't have to? Others before her had forged the way and made God's truth clear to her by the testimony of their transformed lives.

Thank You, Lord, for our deepened confidence in You, because of seeing Your faithfulness in the lives of others. Amen. —J.M.

Be Strong

*Be strong and take heart, all you who hope in the L*ORD.
PSALM 31:24

We hear a lot today about the need of women to be strong, which can bring to mind images of Rosie the Riveter—the poster that has enjoyed renewed popularity since World War II. Its slogan? "We Can Do It!"

How do women "do it"? When Laura's husband left her after many years of marriage, she was devastated. She had never lived alone before, and fear threatened to paralyze her when facing an uncertain future. One day while reading some psalms, the words *Be strong* leaped out at her, and God resonated the words within her.

You're telling me to be strong, aren't You, Lord? In her heart she heard God's unexpected whisper: "*Daniel 10.*" Curious, Laura turned to that chapter and started reading. Verse 19 made her weep in amazement. " 'Do not be afraid, you who are highly esteemed,' he said. 'Peace! Be strong now; be strong.' " When closing her Bible, it fell open to Joshua 1, and Laura's eyes landed on the words "Be strong and very courageous" (v. 7).

In the days and months and years that followed, God's words of "Be strong" echoed in her heart. She heard them when she pulled out the heavy trash can to the curb. She heard them when figuring out her finances. And she heard them when her heart wanted to break yet again: "*Be strong.*"

Our strong and almighty God, thank You
for helping us to "be strong." Amen. —J.M.

The Heart of Hospitality

*Share with the Lord's people who
are in need. Practice hospitality.*

Not counting where you live, where do you feel the most at home?
Perhaps at the home where you can put your feet up and totally relax?
Once you've determined the place, think about what makes you feel
at home there. Is it the charming decor or the embrace of the owner?
Perhaps both?

What does make us feel welcome when we visit others? A warm
and inviting setting can certainly play a role. Cozy can be comforting,
while cold, impersonal surroundings can leave us feeling chilled in spirit.

The key to feeling welcomed in a home resides in the heart of the
hostess. Is she out to impress with her impeccable entertaining or intent
on welcoming her guests with open arms and heart? Entertaining is
pride-based, focused on the hostess, while hospitality is others-based,
focused on the guest.

The hospitable hostess can certainly employ elements of entertaining in order to provide an appealing meal and a delightful occasion.
But she'll also be able to laugh at herself if the soufflé flops. And dusty
furniture won't deter her from asking you to come over for dinner. Her
motivation is to bring joy and care to her guests, who will leave feeling
filled with more than dinner.

*Help us, Lord, to welcome others into our homes with warmth
and joy so they may know Your heart for them. Amen.* —J.M.

Just Say It!

*Do not withhold good from those to whom
it is due, when it is in your power to act.*

PROVERBS 3:27

When Emily was out shopping, she saw an elderly woman with lovely silver hair. They were about to walk by each other, when Emily couldn't resist saying, "Your hair is so beautiful!" The woman's face lit up and a smile wreathed her face. The transformation of her countenance and grateful "Thank you!" imprinted themselves in Emily's memory. Now her motto is "If you think a compliment, say it."

Indeed. Why withhold the opportunity to bring joy to another's day when it's in our power to share some sunshine? Why don't we do that more often?

Consider this: compliments generally come from a confident woman who feels comfortable with herself. Accepting her God-given unique-ness, she isn't caught up in the comparison trap. She knows who she is in Christ and enjoys giving sincere compliments. Insecure people tend to withhold compliments, since they don't feel good about themselves.

We all have days when we're down on ourselves. But let's remember that we are daughters of the King. And as His beloved, we possess the power to lift up other women with just a few words. Yes, if you think a compliment, do say it! You'll feel uplifted too.

*Lord, help us to speak Your love to others and
not withhold good of any kind. Amen.* —J.M.

Our Father

"Abba, Father," he said, "everything is possible for you.
Take this cup from me. Yet not what I will, but what you will."
MARK 14:36

When Jesus prayed in the Garden of Gethsemane, he addressed God with both reverence and intimacy: "Abba, Father." The common thought in Christian circles is that Abba translates as "Daddy" or "Papa." Digging deeper, most scholars don't agree, but they do concur that it's a term expressing warm affection and filial confidence, the confidence of a son or daughter.

Abba has no equivalent in our language, but God's children the world over can know the same confidence in our Father. After a recent visit to Israel, a traveler relayed that she heard children in the streets calling their fathers "Abba." That resonates with us, doesn't it? The word used by children calling to their fathers in Jerusalem is the same word Jesus used in those dark hours before Calvary when calling to His.

Do you need to call out to God today? Do you feel overwhelmed with your life, not knowing which way to turn? Do you want to just give up? Call out to your Abba Father with your deepest heart cry, and He will hear you, His beloved child.

We are honored, our God, to call you Abba, Father,
and we do so with love and praise. Thank You for
always hearing this child of Yours. Amen. —J.M.

Wowed by God

For the Lᴏʀᴅ is the great God, the great King above
all gods. In his hand are the depths of the earth,
and the mountain peaks belong to him.

Pᴀᴀɳᴍ 95:3–4

When you walk with Jesus, when you keep a conversation going with the King of kings, when you see the wonder of His ways, you will likely use one word a lot. That word? *Wow.*

Do you know someone who often says "wow"? Maybe that someone is you? Wow is a word that keeps us from being totally speechless, the word that comes out when we are bowled over by the unexpected.

Think about when that little word escapes your lips. Your wow may be prompted by an astonishing answer to prayer or by a breathtaking sunset. You may say it in exuberance with an exclamation mark, or you may say it in a whisper of holy awe that ends with an ellipsis. Or, you may repeat it over and over when God amazes you by His sweet presence and by His powerful revelations.

So here's an acronym for you: WOW, a Witness of Wonder. You have seen and experienced something so sacred, so inspiring, so miraculous, that all you can say is "Wow."

God, our "Wow!" can be translated as "Praise You!" when
You surprise us with Your wonders. Thank You for Your gifts that
leave us wowed and increase our confidence in You. Amen. —J.M.

God's Waiting Room

*Take delight in the Lord, and he will
give you the desires of your heart.*
PSALM 37:4

One night a woman had a dream in which she saw a word in large letters on a screen: *Waidight*. When she awoke, she was baffled by the unusual word and asked God to reveal its meaning. Instantly He brought to mind how the word was the combination of two: *wait* and *delight*. And just as quickly, the reason for the dream became clear—she was to wait in delight.

Her heart was immediately convicted. She had been waiting on God for a specific promise for years, but she had done so more out of duty not delight. In fact, those years could have been titled "Waiting with Whining." Days had melted into months and months into years, and she didn't understand why she was still waiting for God's answers.

Even now, eighteen years later, she is still waiting; and while it isn't easy, God continues to show His refining purposes—both large and small—while she remains in His waiting room. Delighting herself in God has made all the difference during her stay there.

Are you waiting on God for a desire of your heart? Pray that you can wait with delight, which says to our Lord and the watching world that your trust and confidence are in Him alone.

*Lord, help us to wait in delight while basking
in Your warming light. Amen. —J.M.*

Simply Jesus

In the fear of the LORD there is strong confidence,
and His children will have a place of refuge.
PROVERBS 14:26 NKJV

Google the word *confidence*, and you may be surprised by what awaits you: about 782,000,000 results. Obviously, confidence is a popular topic and apparently an elusive quality that many are seeking. It's no exaggeration to say that there are millions of resources available to those wanting to build their confidence.

Random numbers range online from nine to sixteen steps you need to take to obtain confidence, from both the inside out or the outside in, whichever you prefer. You can even find playlists of songs designed to boost your confidence. Also available? Confidence coaches, confidence by hypnosis, and "8 ways to rebuild your lost confidence." Whew!

And we mustn't overlook all the many images emblazoned with confidence slogans, many of them with women with their arms outstretched toward the sky. Others show knocking the letter *t* off the word *can't*. Just scrolling through the endless sites touting all that self-effort is enough to exhaust us.

What's the better option? Turn to Jesus and look to Him, our one true Source of confidence.

How simple You make it, Lord, to find our
confidence in You alone. Amen. —J.M.

God's "Bucket List"

For to me, to live is Christ and to die is gain.
PHILIPPIANS 1:21

We hear a lot today about keeping a "bucket list"—goals to fulfill before we die. To do things and go places while we still can. The term became popular via the movie by the same name in 2007, and since then the concept has exploded.

Bucket list options abound online, with lists varying in length from 31 to 10,000. You can find forums for hikers and bikers, for Baby Boomers and seniors, and for intrepid travelers and family travelers. There's even a "Bucket List Family" with over a million online followers!

In a video, one hundred people answered the question, "What's on your bucket list?" The wild answers varied widely, as you can imagine, but one young man responded by talking about how he didn't want to die. He wondered aloud if that could go on his bucket list—not dying.

Therein lies the rub. We will die—every one of us—unless Jesus returns before that time. What would God pen for our bucket list between now and then? Why don't we ask Him? Since His list would be made in view of eternity, checking off those choices will give us the most soul satisfaction.

Lord, please pen our earthly bucket list, and help us to remember that it can't begin to compare to what awaits us in heaven. Amen. —J.M.

Our Unfailing God

The LORD delights in those who fear him,
who put their hope in his unfailing love.
PSALM 147:11

True confidence can't be found outside of God. Everything else is false and flimsy and not able to withstand the rigors of life. Yet our confidence can be unflagging when it is rooted in our unfailing Lord.

Think on that word: *unfailing*. Now think about your life, and try to come up with one thing that is *always* unfailing. The task would be much simpler—but more time-consuming—to list the many things that do fail us: the internet connection, appliances and vehicles, government and church leadership, for starters. Add people, and compare your list to the One who isn't even capable of failing us.

The word *unfailing* is found forty-two times in the Bible's New International Version translation, most often to describe God's love and loving-kindness. Other Bible translations use the words *steadfast*, *gracious*, and *loyal*. The dictionary definitions only deepen our understanding: not giving way, not falling short of expectations, completely dependable. The word is also defined as "inexhaustible" and "endless."

When we dwell in the truth of who God is and trust His unfailing love, we can then live in complete confidence of His best desires for us.

Father, we can hardly grasp the concept that You are
incapable of failing us. Thank You for Your unfailing love
that holds us close and will never let us go. Amen. —J.M.

Prayer Talk

Be joyful in hope, patient in affliction, faithful in prayer.
ROMANS 12:12

You may be familiar with the old hymn "Sweet Hour of Prayer." If you're a mom with young children, you may be thinking, *An hour to pray? I'd love to find even five minutes alone to pray without interruption!* Every mom can relate, for sure.

Besides time, what do you yearn for in your prayer life? The subject of prayer is known as an "evergreen topic" in the publishing world, with new books on prayer released regularly. Christians from every generation hunger to improve their prayer lives. What would make it more meaningful? Sadly, time spent with God is too often seen as one more thing to check off the daily to-do list.

The secret is to view prayer as a dialogue with your dearest friend. It's not a duty to perform but a delight to enjoy. Yes, we can talk with Jesus throughout our day, but a few moments set apart each day allow us to *listen* to our loving Lord.

When we do that, our relationship with Him will deepen and our confidence in Him will increase. And just imagine the difference those times will make when we meet Jesus in heaven. We won't be greeting a stranger but our beloved Savior, and our sweet conversations will continue forever!

Thank You, Lord, that the better we know You here, the greater our anticipation and joy to meet You face-to-face. Amen. —J.M.

Our Giving God

*Every good gift and every perfect gift is from above,
and comes down from the Father of lights, with
whom there is no variation or shadow of turning.*

JAMES 1:17 NKJV

What's the most memorable gift you've ever received? Was it wrapped in shiny paper or in love alone? Think about these examples to trigger your own: the gift of a meal after a surgery or baby's birth, child care or housecleaning when life overwhelmed, a flowering plant to cheer during dark days.

Our God originated the custom of giving amazing gifts. Verse after beautiful verse reminds us of God's extravagant heart. Hear of His gifts with new ears:

- For the wages of sin is death; but the *gift* of God is eternal life through Jesus Christ our Lord. (Romans 6:23 KJV)
- For by grace are ye saved through faith; and that not of yourselves: it is the *gift* of God. (Ephesians 2:8 KJV, emphasis added)

The next time you see the words *John 3:16* emblazoned on a banner at a sporting event, think of it as a present to the watching world. "For God so loved the world, that he gave his only begotten Son, that whosoever believeth in him should not perish, but have everlasting life" (KJV).

How can our hearts not respond like Paul's? "Thanks be unto God for his unspeakable gift" (2 CORINTHIANS 9:15 KJV).

Our Father, thank You for the gift of Jesus. Amen. —J.M.

Your Hand in His

"Truly I tell you, anyone who will not receive the kingdom of God like a little child will never enter it."

LUKE 18:17

What does a confident woman look like to you? Does someone you know come to mind with that question? Now evaluate the components of that woman's confidence. Is it found in the exteriors of her life—her attractiveness, a handsome husband, a lovely home—or does it emanate from within?

Confidence that is constructed with things alone will eventually crumble or at least fade like the paint on a sun-beaten house. Now think of a woman who radiates the beauty of a peaceful heart because her confidence is based in Christ. She knows the One who loves her and has learned that the fiercest of troubles cannot wrest her from His loving arms.

This woman's life is founded in our Lord, and she lives in the assurance of His care for her. She knows freedom from the stresses and strains of life because she turns over each one to her Savior. She is content to be a child of God whose hand remains in His, knowing He will never fail her trusting heart.

Picture yourself as a child holding God's hand or resting in His arms. The simplicity and serenity of that scene will display itself in you as a confident woman whose faith resides in her loving Father.

Lord, we are content and blessed to be
Your children—praise You! Amen. —J.M.

A Fine Line

*Even to your old age and gray hairs
I am he, I am he who will sustain you.
I have made you and I will carry you;
I will sustain you and I will rescue you.*

ISAIAH 46:4

Do you find yourself checking for new gray hairs or wrinkles these days? Or perhaps your hair has already turned white or is covered with dye? In our youth-oriented culture, our natural confidence can dwindle as our birthday candles increase. Appearance carries more weight in our society—and often with us—than we'd care to admit.

See if this is true for you. When your skin is taut and muscles firm, your confidence register rises. Conversely, sags and age spots cause your confidence level to plummet. Yes, skin-deep beauty and the natural confidence of youth wane as we get older.

Yet our Lord will gladly give us a sustaining confidence in exchange for anything natural we find in ourselves. In fact, those fine lines on our faces can remind us to see the fine line between pride and confidence. The key factor is the source. Pride is found in the shallows of self. Confidence beautified by humility is found in Christ alone.

*Thank You, Lord, for the beauty of
Your sustaining confidence. Amen. —J.M.*

The Ultimate Gift

*"For the eyes of the Lord are on the righteous and his
ears are attentive to their prayer, but the face
of the Lord is against those who do evil."*

1 PETER 3:12

You've heard this comment: "I wish I could do something to help, but I'll pray." Did you catch the absurdity behind that statement? "Since I can't do anything else, I'll have to pray." Prayer is often looked on as the last resort, a pitiful offering, compared to giving something physical when someone is in need.

Have we forgotten that prayer is the ultimate gift? Out of prayer floods the potent flow of power and life and healing. Wellsprings of wonders are found in our incomparable God, the One who hears our every prayer. Compare that to the "positive thoughts" and "energy" sent to someone dealing with difficulties. Where is the power in those well-meaning words? When we revere and enjoy the privilege of prayer, lives will be transformed, including our own.

Yes, it is good and necessary to meet real needs, but let's always begin with prayer. And when we tell someone we'll pray for them, let's make sure to do just that—and also to come alongside them when we can. But our best gift to them happens while on our knees.

*Impress on us anew, Father, the power
and privilege of prayer. Amen.* —J.M.

Our Faithful God

Because of the LORD's great love we are not consumed,
for his compassions never fail. They are new every
morning; great is your faithfulness.

LAMENTATIONS 3:22–23

Your friend was late—again—to meet you for lunch. You forgot to RSVP to the wedding of your best friend's son. Your sister canceled a road trip you'd been looking forward to for ages. Our laments could fill pages of a yellow legal pad with the times others have flaked out on us—or when we've been the flake.

Are you familiar with the slang term *flake*? When a flake has nothing to do with snow, it usually means "an unreliable person." Most people would prefer not to be known as "a flake"—especially if they struggle with dandruff!

But seriously, our humanness means we will forget appointments, disappoint others, and generally mess up. While some folks rightfully wear the "flaky" moniker more than others, we've all had our moments of unreliability. The good news? God is *never* flaky. In fact, He's quite the opposite; He's faithful. If God needed a middle name, Faithful would be fitting.

Lift your voice and spirits by singing the hymn "Great Is Thy Faithfulness," inspired by today's verse. And be grateful that while the best of us can be flaky, our God is ever faithful.

Thank You, Father, that You are faithful to love us, faithful to hear
our prayers, and faithful to keep Your promises. Amen. —J.M.

Don't Forget to Remember

I will remember the works of the LORD;
Surely I will remember Your wonders of old.

PSALM 77:11 NKJV

Twila, a divorced woman with grown children, struggles now and then to remain upbeat, because right now the script of her life differs from her desires. She loves the Lord and enjoys a sweet relationship with Him, but now and then the realities of her life—having to do everything, missing companionship, traveling solo—make her want to sing the blues.

That's when she knows it's time for a memory check. She looks back over her life and recounts all that God has done for her and thanks Him all over again. The memories of God's faithfulness are many, but the remembrance of His sweetest miracle always sets Twila's heart to singing.

Years earlier, one of her beloved sons got caught up in drugs, traveling a downward path to meth addiction. Her son's suicide attempt while drunk was the wake-up call needed to seek help. One miracle after another unfolded, beginning with the Christian rehab center God provided. More miracles: graduating from a Christian college with honors, becoming a husband and father, and working his way up to a leadership position within a Christian company.

What workings and wonders of God do you need to remember today to encourage you in whatever is facing you now?

Thank You, Lord, for the blessing of memory so that
we can recall Your amazing faithfulness. Amen. —J.M.

Not for Sale

I praise you because I am fearfully and wonderfully made; your works are wonderful, I know that full well.
PSALM 139:14

A young teen girl confided in her mom, "Sometimes my friends hurt my feelings. Like, they make fun of what I'm wearing all the time because it's not from the mall. I don't really care though." She let that last sentence hang in the air, and her sad tone betrayed her brave words.

Remembering what it was like to be thirteen and full of insecurity, her mom shared with her daughter what she wished she could go back and tell her awkward, permed, nerdy middle-school self: confidence is something you can't find in a store in the mall.

She reminded her girl of how fearless she was as a young second grader, choosing to wear her hair short and selecting one-of-a-kind outfits each day that made her stand out, not fit in. Her mom admitted how she had often wished for that sense of style and natural, easy confidence as a child. Her daughter smiled, warmed by her mother's admission and affirmations.

Since the insecurities of that teen girl may still reside within us, let's take to heart that mom's wise words and remind ourselves of God's truths: we are wonderfully made. We are chosen. We are of great value. We are uniquely gifted. We are fiercely loved.

Lord, help us to see ourselves as You see us:
cherished and adored. Amen. —J.M.

All These Things

Yet in all these things we are more than conquerors through Him who loved us.

ROMANS 8:37 NKJV

What makes up the list of "all these things" in your life that need to be conquered? What stresses of life are pressing in on you today? Here's the apostle Paul's sobering list of "all these things" found in Romans 8:35 (NIV): trouble, hardship, persecution, famine, nakedness, danger, and sword.

People like us, throughout all generations, have experienced challenging trials of every ilk. Yet no matter what heading our troubles fall under, the timeless truth of God remains: through Him we can overcome whatever is facing us.

Let's hear that truth in the various translations of God's Word so that it will transform our thinking about our troubles today. Through God who loves us, we gain a "sweeping victory," a victory that is "overwhelming, surpassing, complete." The descriptions of our victory continue: full, triumphant, and glorious.

Are you seeing the magnitude and magnificence of what is available to us in our God who loves us beyond measure? Take heart that we are "superconquerors" and "more than winners" with our Lord and that we will "prevail completely" and "overcome strongly." Yes, we will "always taste victory" through God who loves us.

Put your list of troubles next to God's truths, and trust His overcoming power in "all these things."

Father, when my troubles want to overtake me, may I be overwhelmed by one thing alone: Your loving care for me. Amen. —J.M.

Lifting Up Jesus

"And I, if I am lifted up from the earth,
will draw all peoples to Myself."
JOHN 12:32 NKJV

In our culture of YouTube and selfies, the craving for fame has eclipsed all else in the lives of many. Performance is paramount. Showing off has become the norm. Perhaps you've seen that mentality creep into churches, often turning sanctuaries into entertainment and performance venues. Yes, the name of Jesus is drummed and sung, but are our hearts centered on Jesus or on that attractive guy or gal leading worship?

Contrast that with the rare church where the choir sings from the back of the sanctuary, without a face to be seen. The singers focus on lifting up God, while the listeners focus on the rich words and music meant to bring worship and praise to God. Even the congregational singing is often led by the pianist from the back of the church.

While *unshowmanlike* isn't a word the dictionary recognizes, it is an unusual word and idea. It brings to mind its close cousin—*humility*—and the value God places on that trait. In fact, it reminds us of the words of Jesus' cousin, John the Baptist: "He must increase, but I must decrease" (John 3:30 NKJV). While *unshowmanlike* isn't technically a word, the concept gives us something to consider, doesn't it?

Lord, we pray to lift You up in our worship and in our lives
so that You alone will be seen and glorified. Amen. —J.M.

Safe

Google the words *safety products*, and you'll see over two billion results. No, that isn't a typo—over two *billion*. Keeping safe is a high priority, and people will take extravagant measures to feel secure in what often feels like a scary world. The crime rate where we reside can contribute to our sense of security—or lack of it.

But the fanciest alarm systems in our homes and the flashiest safety features in our vehicles can't guarantee our safety in an unsafe society and imperfect world. Often the precautions taken only give us a false sense of security. Fanny Crosby's hymn, "Safe in the Arms of Jesus," written in 1868, includes the words "safe from corroding care." Yes, safety is desired in every realm of life, even from the niggling worries that keep us awake at night.

Our ultimate safety depends upon God. While we would be wise to avoid rickety ladders and driving too fast, we also don't want to be paranoid and allow fear to rob our lives of joy. We can't control catastrophic events ranging from floods and earthquakes to random shootings, but we can know God's peace in such a way that our sleep will be sweet.

*Father, help us to live in serenity, knowing
our soul safety is solely in You. Amen. —J.M.*

Real Love

This is real love—not that we loved God, but that he loved us and sent his Son as a sacrifice to take away our sins. Dear friends, since God loved us that much, we surely ought to love each other.
1 JOHN 4:10–11 NLT

The admonition in 1 John that we surely "ought" to love each other can also read as "should" and that we "owe" that kind of love to others. The truth is we can't consistently love like that with our human limitations. Only God can fill us with the kind of love necessary to love the unlovable, the disagreeable, the ones who have wounded us deeply.

A mom watching TV news bemoaned the tragic death of a child, speaking aloud her sadness for the family's sorrow. Her junior-high son was mystified. "Mom, you don't even know those people. Why do you care?" Why? Because God had filled her with love for others whether she knew them or not.

Perhaps you know people who committed their lives to Jesus as adults. If so, you may have heard them express their surprise at experiencing a newfound love for people—even for those they previously couldn't stand. Why? They had felt God's embrace and instantly knew that "since God loved me that much," how could they do any less? How can we?

Help us, dear Lord, to remember anew Your love for us on the cross, so we will gladly and gratefully love others. Amen. —J.M.

Busy Beavers

Yes, my soul, find rest in God; my hope comes from him. Truly he is my rock and my salvation; he is my fortress, I will not be shaken.
PSALM 62:5–6

Have you noticed what people say when you ask them, "How are you?" Usually it's this little word: *busy*. *Fine* has fallen by the wayside, and *busy* has jumped up to take its place. While there are exceptions, most are prone today to give that typical response, perhaps even reciting all their reasons for being so busy.

Wearing the "Busy" badge as an indicator of our worth has wormed its way into our thinking. If we're not careening from one car pool to the next or hitting the gym before work, then we may fall short of enough "busy-worthy" activities in our lives.

In our more sane moments, we long to hop off the treadmill, but our inner busy beaver fears to be seen as a slovenly sloth. Our calendars are so filled that we struggle to fit in a quick lunch with a dear friend. Since when are we worth more by doing more? What are we out to prove?

Take a deep breath. Look at your life with the lens you'll use when your story reads "The End." And then pray for wisdom on how to replace your "Busy" badge with a "Loving My Life!" button.

Lord, help us to rest in the truth that our worth comes from You not from how much we do. Amen. —J.M.

Counting Hairs

*Are not five sparrows sold for two pennies? Yet not one of them
is forgotten by God. Indeed, the very hairs of your head are all
numbered. Don't be afraid; you are worth more than many sparrows.*

Luke 12:6–7

Thick or thin, long or short, blond or blue, the hairs on our heads are
known by God in their exact number. Have you thought about that? Let's
take a look at God's challenge of keeping track of that ever-changing
statistic.

According to trichologists (trained scalp experts), we lose between
50 to 100 hairs a day. No wonder you often pull hair out of your brush
and use a "hair snare" for the shower drain, right? Amazingly, we each
have about 100,000 scalp hairs that follow a predictable growth cycle
of three phases: growing, stopping growth, and resting. (You can find
the technical names for those stages online, if you're curious!) *Alopecia*
is the medical term for normal hair loss, which occurs because of the
growth cycles.

So why the hair lesson? Simply because it demonstrates God's
amazing knowledge of us. The number of our tresses never remains the
same! The next time you sigh over hair you've shed, you can wonder
what new number is on your "heavenly hair chart." And you can be
grateful for God's amazing interest in everything about you, down to
every hair on your head!

*God, Your detailed knowledge of us is
awesome—thank You! Amen. —J.M.*

Got Regret?

*For the kind of sorrow God wants us to experience
leads us away from sin and results in salvation. There's
no regret for that kind of sorrow. But worldly sorrow,
which lacks repentance, results in spiritual death.*

2 CORINTHIANS 7:10 NLT

"Godly sorrow" that leads us to repentance and faith in Christ is good.
Yet many Christians live in the chokehold of life-draining regrets. Are you
one of them? Do you find yourself rehearsing the "if onlys" of your life
rather than rejoicing in your relationship with Christ? Regrets rob us of
the joy of today and taint our hopes for the future. Regrets also undermine our confidence. The solution? The truth of God's Word.

Hold on to this:

*GOD makes everything come out right; he puts victims back
on their feet. He showed Moses how he went about his work,
opened up his plans to all Israel. GOD is sheer mercy and
grace; not easily angered, he's rich in love. He doesn't end-
lessly nag and scold, nor hold grudges forever. He doesn't
treat us as our sins deserve, nor pay us back in full for our
wrongs. As high as heaven is over the earth, so strong is his
love to those who fear him. And as far as sunrise is from sunset, he has separated us from our sins. Psalm 103:6–12 (MSG)*

*Lord, we choose to live in Your truth and refuse to let regrets
strangle us from living a life of freedom in You. Amen. —J.M.*

Imposters Anonymous

With your help I can advance against a troop;
with my God I can scale a wall.
PSALM 18:29

A woman tells the story of when she auditioned for a community chorus. "I'd been singing for years, but this group stretched me in many ways as I stepped outside the 'bubble' of my church choir and worship team." The first couple of months, she felt in over her head and feared she'd be told she didn't qualify after all.

By the end of her first year, however, her fears were allayed. "I was so glad I stuck it out! I'd grown as a singer, made new friends, and gained confidence." The happy singer celebrated this milestone in a blog post, eventually seen by the entire chorus. The most common comment that ensued surprised her: "I was terrified my first year too!"

The director told her, "Your anxiety didn't show." The responses reminded her of the truth we all need to remember. All of us struggle with confidence at one time or another. Some of us just get really good at hiding it. In moments—or months!—of insecurity, we may often feel like the only imposters in the room. But when we fess up and admit our feelings of inadequacy, others will gladly join us with shared relief and joy.

God, with all our differences, You made us so much alike. Give us the courage to be real and foster real relationships. Amen. —J.M.

Headed for Home

*My Father's house has many rooms; if that were not so, would I
have told you that I am going there to prepare a place for you?
And if I go and prepare a place for you, I will come back and
take you to be with me that you also may be where I am.*

JOHN 14:2–3

Picture a long timeline with a straight line that runs as far as your eyes can
see. Now envision a tiny dot on that line, so small it's barely visible. There
you have it, the speck that represents our lives, just a little blip, really.

Each one of us believers in Christ is headed toward our last breath
that will usher us into our heavenly home. We're not prone to think
about that truth much, are we? But it's a reality that we can await with
full confidence and God's peace, based on God's Word.

The world doesn't possess that same peace. A radio announcer
hosting a country music countdown played "Everything's Gonna Be
Alright" as sung by Kenny Chesney. When the tune ended, the radio
host commented in a wistful voice, "I want to believe that." We all want
to believe that, don't we? And as followers of Christ we can. We can
have confidence that everything will be all right because God keeps
His promises.

*Thank You, Jesus, that the best part of Your promise
of heaven is that we will be with You. Amen. —J.M.*

Morning Matters

*Very early in the morning, while it was still dark, Jesus got up,
left the house and went off to a solitary place, where he prayed.*

MARK 1:35

Do you ever feel paralyzed by fear? So wanting to do the right thing that often you default to no action at all? That mode of living causes us to stumble through life in confusion rather than stride through life with confidence.

Begin each day with our Lord, and seek His agenda and schedule. Lay every concern of your day before Him, and then listen to what He has to say. Yes, your to-do list will try to crowd out God's voice, so keep a notebook handy to write down all the things you need to remember. That way your mind will be freed to focus on hearing from Your Father.

Morning time with God will calm your mind and heart and allow Him to reveal His best plans for your day. He may bring a lonely widowed neighbor to mind who needs a visit or phone call. Maybe take her an extra plate of dinner or a treat? God may remind you of a faraway friend whose mom recently died, and you determine to send a sympathy card. Or he may nudge you to pen a note asking forgiveness, even while in your posture of prayer.

*Help us to seek Your divine help at the beginning of each day, Lord,
so that You will be seen and glorified in our lives. Amen. —J.M.*

What's in a Name?

"She will give birth to a son, and you are to give him the name Jesus, because he will save his people from their sins."

MATTHEW 1:21

If you're a parent, you probably spent hours poring over names in baby books to come up with the perfect, fitting name for your child. Or you may have waited until after your child's birth to get a sense of the best name for your newborn. You probably considered the sound of it and the possible nicknames you'd either abhor or adore.

For many parents the meaning of the name may carry the most influence in their decision. The importance of names is all throughout scripture. Remember how Abraham and Sarah named their miracle son Isaac, meaning "laughter"? Although we have to wonder if today's parents know that Cameron means "crooked nose"!

Our God goes by powerful names in scripture with meanings that apply to no other. Linger over each one, and be reminded afresh of the One we can trust completely:

Adonai: the God who is in charge
El Elyon: the Most High God
El Olam: the Everlasting God
El Shaddai: the Almighty God
Yahweh: the God who is always there

*Father, we marvel at the capabilities revealed in
Your names and how they resonate within us,
causing deepened confidence in You. Amen. —J.M.*

Looking to Jesus

Looking unto Jesus, the author and finisher of our faith, who for the joy that was set before Him endured the cross, despising the shame, and has sat down at the right hand of the throne of God.

HEBREWS 12:2 NKJV

A writer stood in her community church and requested prayer for a pressing writing deadline and mentioned the monumental amount of work facing her. An out-of-town trip and other obligations had already encroached on her writing time. She felt compelled to share, since she knew their intercessory prayers would make all the difference.

After the service several people let her know they'd be praying for her. She expected the same kind of response when the teacher of the women's weekly Bible study approached her. The woman questioned the amount of work that still needed to be done in two weeks, and with a smile and shake of her head said, "Honey, it ain't gonna happen!"

While her words surprised the writer, they didn't discourage her. She'd seen God provide many times and was confident He'd come through for her again. Simply because of who He is: faithful.

Have others discouraged you when you pursued what God called you to do? Even the best of Christians sometimes fail to encourage us. That's when it's crucial to look to Christ, the Author and Finisher of our faith—and of writing projects!

We're looking to You, Jesus, to be faithful
to the finish line. Thank You! Amen. —J.M.

Happy as Kings

Sing to the LORD with thanksgiving;
Sing praises on the harp to our God,
Who covers the heavens with clouds,
Who prepares rain for the earth,
Who makes grass to grow on the mountains.
PSALM 147:7–8 NKJV

See if your heart soars when you read these lines by Scottish writer and children's author Robert Louis Stevenson:

"The world is so full of a number of things,
I'm sure we should all be as happy as kings."

We don't have to be children to revel in the "number of things" God has given us for our enjoyment. Lilacs in springtime. The glorious foliage of fall. A diamond-studded snowscape. A tiny flower pushing its way through a crack in the sidewalk. Cumulus clouds in whimsical shapes. The sound of the wind in the trees.

When Sarah met her future husband's mother for the first time, she was struck by her appreciation for the little things of life. She later told her, "I remember how you commented about the fresh scent after the rain." She still enjoys her mother-in-love's pleasure in the simple joys that nature offers us.

Our delight in God's world is another way to connect with our Creator. When a sweeping sunset takes our breath away or a darting lizard makes us grin, let's send up a prayer of joyful thanks, shall we?

Our Creator God, when we see the amazing works of Your hands,
we know we can trust those very hands. Amen. —J.M.

A Community of Caring

Some men came, bringing to him a paralyzed man, carried by four of them. Since they could not get him to Jesus because of the crowd, they made an opening in the roof above Jesus by digging through it and then lowered the mat the man was lying on.

MARK 2:3–4

Let's envision the story about the paralytic man. Four friends carried him—who knows how far—and then couldn't get through the door to Jesus. But that didn't deter them. They dug their own door through the roof and didn't mind getting dirty to do it. After all, they were his friends, and they were determined to get help for him.

Rose lived alone, and when she put out her back, she could barely move. Her friends became her hands and feet. They brought food and served her meals in bed. They picked up painkillers and groceries for her. They even came over at all hours to help walk her to the bathroom. In her suffering, Rose was comforted by God's love in the actions of her friends.

When our lives go awry because of an accident, sudden illness, or a death in the family, the support of others keeps us afloat. Community is God's gift to us, both in the giving and receiving. Within that community our confidence in God and one another grows.

Because of Your care for us, Lord, we are blessed to care for others and also accept their care. Amen. —J.M.

Time Wise

Be very careful, then, how you live—not as unwise but as wise,
making the most of every opportunity, because the days are evil.
Therefore do not be foolish, but understand what the Lord's will is.

EPHESIANS 5:15–17

Here's a riddle for you: I can crawl, and I can fly. I have hands, but I have no legs or wings. What am I? Did you figure it out? The answer is *time,* and it's obvious that riddle was written before digital clocks were invented!

In spite of all our modern conveniences to save time, we seem to have less of it. For many, time has become a more precious commodity than money. Time management is a hot topic, with over two billion hits on Google.

Do you often feel selfish regarding your time? Do interruptions in your schedule cause you to grit your teeth in annoyance? What if we were able to view interruptions as God's interventions instead? To see them as opportunities to show His love and grace?

When we allow God to oversee our minutes, He expands them to encompass His every purpose. So the next time a friend or neighbor calls or stops by in need of a listening ear, or a child is pestering you for attention, you can choose to relish or resent the intrusion. Entrust God with your time, and taste the delights of His divine timetable.

Lord, our lives—and our every minute—are Yours. Amen. —J.M.

Unlikely?

*"For my thoughts are not your thoughts,
neither are your ways my ways," declares the L*ORD.
ISAIAH 55:8

Are you looking at a longing in your life that is unlikely to happen? When something is deemed unlikely, it is improbable, an outcome marked by doubt. That dismal word of *unlikely* also foresees little prospect of success, so you may as well erase that hope of yours as unpromising and likely to fail.

Let's turn that ominous word to *optimistic* by reviewing accounts in the Bible. We'd all agree that it was unlikely for the Red Sea and the Jordan River to be parted for God's children to cross on dry land. And how likely is it that a donkey would talk to its obstinate master, Balaam? It was also unlikely for a boy's lunch to feed thousands—and have umpteen leftovers!

Now look at your "unlikely" through the lens of God's Word. Place it next to God's promises. Read His words of hope and love, and believe them. Unlikely stories are everywhere! The parents of Nick Vujicic surely thought it was unlikely that their son, born without arms and legs, would speak to millions around the world about Christ, marry, and have children. Or that his hobbies would include fishing, painting, and swimming! Unlikely, indeed!

*Lord, only You can change an "unlikely" to a
resounding reality—thank You! Amen. —J.M.*

Living to Die

Those who walk uprightly enter into peace;
they find rest as they lie in death.

ISAIAH 57:2

Historic cemeteries take us down a path of time, exciting lovers of history and sobering others as to the brevity of this life. When reading the names and epitaphs on leaning grave markers, one can't help but wonder, *Who were these people? What were their hopes and dreams? Did they love and know love?* Like us, they breathed the air of this earth, ate and slept, laughed and cried, worked and played.

They are gone, but we are still here in this tenuous swath of time. What will our legacy be? Besides a marker, what will we leave behind that will testify to God's grace in our lives? We all long to know our lives are valued and worthwhile, but do we endeavor to live in a way that will make an eternal difference?

In a rural churchyard cemetery, a towering tombstone draws attention to itself, bidding visitors to read the inscription: "Behold as you pass by, as you be now, so once was I; as I be now, so you must be. Prepare for death and follow me." That truth may make us squirm, but it's truth nevertheless. We need to live, knowing we will die. What better way to "prepare for death" than to "walk uprightly"?

Lord, may our fleeting days only fuel our desire
to live more fully for You and others. Amen. —J.M.

Our Father's Love

"And the LORD, He is the One who goes before you. He will be with you, He will not leave you nor forsake you; do not fear nor be dismayed."

DEUTERONOMY 31:8 NKJV

The video went viral of the young ballerina in her pink tutu—and in hysterics at her first performance. The teacher onstage with the class couldn't calm her, and her screams crescendoed over the music. Then from backstage strode her daddy with a baby in one arm and his other arm extended to his daughter.

Holding her daddy's hand, her cries ceased, while her father stayed onstage with her, his khaki shorts and black T-shirt quite the contrast to the lineup of pink. He not only stayed with his daughter, but also did the ballet moves with her—as well as he could with a baby in one arm! His little ballerina remained calm with her daddy by her side, and he cast off the need to be cool as he twirled and danced with her. Her need for him outweighed his concern about anything else; his only thought was for his daughter.

What a beautiful picture of our heavenly Father and His tender care toward us. Whatever our struggle, He's there with us. Whenever we are fearful, maybe even crying hysterically, He is there extending His hand of love toward us. His calmness becomes our calmness as He draws us close to Himself.

Thank You, Father, for always staying near. Amen. —J.M.

Behold the Butterfly!

*"Behold, the former things have come to pass, and new things
I declare; before they spring forth I tell you of them."*

ISAIAH 42:9 NKJV

Elizabeth stepped out her front door to get the mail and almost ran into the swallowtail butterfly swooping across her walkway. She smiled as she watched it sail by her mailbox and on down the street. The cause of her smile ran deeper, however, since the butterfly is one of God's reminders for His promised new days in her life—days she had been awaiting by faith for almost twenty years.

The metamorphosis of a caterpillar into a beautiful butterfly is astounding to observe. After eating its egg, the caterpillar, also called larva, eats leaves constantly until it's one hundred times its size. The Smithsonian Institute uses animation to show all the changes during the chrysalis stage before the caterpillar is transformed into a butterfly. Such an amazing example of our amazing God!

Maybe you are in the darkness of a confining cocoon right now. You wonder if anything will ever change or if God even hears your prayers. Remember the caterpillar, friend, and know that our almighty God of infinite care can make all things new for you. Feed on His Word while you are waiting in the shadows, so you can emerge ready to embrace the new days God has prepared for you.

*Thank You, God, for the beautiful new
days found only in You. Amen. —J.M.*

Confidence in Our King

I will extol You, my God, O King; and I will bless Your name
forever and ever. . . . I will meditate on the glorious splendor
of Your majesty, and on Your wondrous works.
PSALM 145:1, 5 NKJV

The world has been swept up by Great Britain's royal weddings for decades, with every detail examined before, during, and after the resplendent event. Movies and television shows based on the royal family also have captured wide audiences.

Our more casual North American population is fascinated by royal protocol. When meeting the queen, a visitor is to address her as "Your Majesty" and subsequently refer to her as "Ma'am." The centuries-old tradition of backing out of a room has been modified by Queen Elizabeth in the interest of safety and is now required of only two members of the royal household.

Yet only God qualifies as true royalty, the one King worthy of the highest adulation. The word *extol* that King David used means to "praise highly" and "exalt." Psalm 29:4 tells us that the voice of the Lord is "powerful" and "full of majesty." And these words from Revelation 19:16 ring with the music of Handel's *Messiah*: "King of kings and lord of lords." How can we not have confidence in the majestic One who loves us supremely?

As hymn writer Harriet Buell wrote in 1877, "All glory to God, I'm a child of the King."

Our royal and almighty King, how we
praise and worship You! Amen. —J.M.

A Wise Life

Teach us to number our days,
that we may gain a heart of wisdom.
PSALM 90:12

A few years after Jeri's marriage ended, her father died. She and her mom now lived alone, a state away, and they talked every day on the phone. Her mom often commented on the quick passage of time, saying, "Every year goes faster," and Jeri had to agree. They often reminisced, with daughter Jeri writing down family history and stories she didn't want to forget.

And then with very little warning, her mom's days were numbered, and Jeri was grateful to be with her the last weeks of her life. She treasured their rich conversations, and she videotaped some of her mom's storytelling. She held those precious moments pressed against her heart, knowing they would soon be memories only.

Her mom's home-going to heaven has deepened Jeri's commitment to infuse each day with intentional living instead of mindlessly being swept along by the currents of her circumstances. She longs to live fully, prayerfully focused on God's intents for her life.

Not to be morbid, but perhaps looking at our lives under a motivating "What if I had only one month left to live?" would give us a perspective otherwise ignored. The tyranny of the urgent would fall away to reveal the important, would it not?

Lord, please show us daily Your desires
for this life You've given us. Amen. —J.M.

Unsearchable

Oh, the depth of the riches both of the wisdom and knowledge of God! How unsearchable are His judgments and His ways past finding out!

ROMANS 11:33 NKJV

Nanette's niece was studying to be a doctor when they engaged in a conversation during a vacation that included a visit to an iconic book-store. Both believers, they enjoyed perusing the many books, new and used, in the religious section. Banter went back and forth regarding favorite authors and recommendations, but then the conversation turned when Nanette made a comment about appreciating the mystery of God.

Her niece's look of dismay was conveyed in her voice. "Actually, I have a hard time with that about God. I like facts and figures, and I want everything laid out. I want to know why He does something, and it frustrates me when I don't."

Nanette understood her niece's heart, for years before she herself had harangued God one night with questions that plagued her—situations that begged for understanding. When she finally grew silent, she heard God's quiet voice in her heart. *"I don't require your understanding. I only require your trust. Can you trust Me even when you don't understand?"*

These words written by William Cowper in 1774 still resound: "God moves in a mysterious way His wonders to perform."

When we don't understand, God, we choose to trust You, our loving and good God. Amen. —J.M.

The Prayers of Many

*He has delivered us from such a deadly peril, and he will
deliver us again. On him we have set our hope that he
will continue to deliver us, as you help us by your prayers.
Then many will give thanks on our behalf for the gracious
favor granted us in answer to the prayers of many.*

2 CORINTHIANS 1:10–11

Over the phone from Florida to California, Jen poured out her heart to
her friend Abby about the hardness of her life. The hopelessness in Jen's
voice moved Abby to say, "Reach out to the prayer warriors in your life
and ask them to pray for you. You need an outpouring of prayer right
now." She also encouraged Jen to be in the Word.

The next morning Jen texted what God was showing her, and the
tone of her texts was devoid of the despair of the day before. She had
contacted ten people to pray for her, and not only were they praying,
but they were also sending her notes of encouragement.

Why are we often reticent to ask others to pray for us, even apol-
ogizing for "bothering them"? The saying "Prayer changes things"
isn't just a cliché for home decor—it's truth. Behind every movement of
God's hand is the power of prayer. The greatest gift we can give one
another is the gift of intercession, so let's be generous to pray for one
another and grateful to receive that blessing.

Lord, help us not to hesitate to ask for prayer. Amen. —J.M.

The Beauty of Belonging

And you are Christ's, and Christ is God's.
1 Corinthians 3:23 NKJV

When we introduce a relative of ours, we often say, "I'd like you to meet my son, my sister, my father"—you get the idea. We use the possessive pronoun of "my" to show they belong to us. They're part of our family. We belong to our family members like no other.

God has given us an innate sense of needing to belong. We see that need fulfilled in groups of all kinds—from local gangs to book clubs. The organizations are endless that require membership to "belong."

Yet there is nothing as satisfying and beautiful as knowing we belong to Jesus. Two beautiful hymns portray the joy and promise of that belonging: "Now I Belong to Jesus" by Norman J. Clayton and "I Am His, and He Is Mine" by George W. Robinson. If you want a blessing, go online and find videos and lyrics of both hymns.

Because of the blood of Christ, we belong in His eternal family. That bond overshadows any earthly family, whether by blood or otherwise. God will never disown us, for as Robinson's hymn says, "In a love which cannot cease, I am His, and He is mine."

How grateful we are to belong to You, dear Jesus! Amen. —J.M.

The Way to Obey

Then they said, "Let's call the young woman and ask her about it." So they called Rebekah and asked her, "Will you go with this man?" "I will go," she said.
Genesis 24:57–58

Read the story of Isaac and Rebekah as found in Genesis 24, and enjoy this beautiful account of God's faithfulness. Abraham's loyal servant played a key role. His specific prayer of receiving water for himself and his camels from God's designated woman was answered before his final words had left his lips. Before he had finished praying, "Rebekah came out, with her jar on her shoulder"(v. 45).

Not only did Rebekah fulfill what the servant had requested from God, she also went beyond his prayer, offering accommodations for the man and his camels. Then the man bowed down and worshipped the Lord with praise, who had "not abandoned his kindness and faithfulness to my master" (v. 27).

Rebekah heard the servant's praise to God and then learned the full story before dinner of how she was his answer to prayer for a wife for Isaac. Her relatives confirmed, "This is from the LORD" (v. 50) and that the Lord had "directed" (v. 51) for Rebekah to become Isaac's wife. She was immediately obedient to God's obvious workings. The very next day she left the only life she knew to journey 700 miles by camel to be the wife of a man she had never met.

Lord, give us confident hearts of obedience like Rebekah's. Amen. —J.M.

Kiwis and Kangaroos

God saw all that he had made, and it was very good.
GENESIS 1:31

Our Creator obviously loves variety in all realms of life. Fruit from kiwis to cantaloupes, flowers from roses to peonies, animals from lions to kangaroos. We could go on and on, with trees from oak to palm, vegetables from corn to green beans, birds from jays to finches.

Think of the array of colors He uses to paint His creations. Not just one shade of green, but everything from lime to forest green. The hues He chooses burst with His creativity, from pink flamingos to yellow daffodils. Don't forget the myriad sounds and flavors that saturate our lives with enjoyment: the robin's call and a running brook, sour lemons and sweet strawberries.

When we examine how many varieties make up the strata of God's creative hand, the numbers are staggering. For example, close to a million different kinds of insects have been identified, but entomologists estimate the species range from two to thirty million!

The greatest example of God's penchant for variance is *us*, the ones made in His image. Billions of people, and yet no two exactly alike—just like snowflakes and seashells. Mind boggling, isn't it? So today when you look in the mirror, see and appreciate what God sees—His one and only you, beloved of Him.

God, we praise You for Your boundless creativity and pray to appreciate more than ever the masterpieces You have made—including the one reading these words. Amen. —J.M.

Feel God's Pleasure

*Thou art worthy, O Lord, to receive glory and honour
and power: for thou hast created all things,
and for thy pleasure they are and were created.*

REVELATION 4:11 KJV

Just as God's creativity pleases us, our creativity pleases Him. Think of the joy you feel when immersed in your favorite creative endeavor, and then liken that to the pleasure God felt when He designed each of us. Imagine His thoughts: *Hmm, I'll give her an artistic eye, this one a talent for problem solving, and that child of Mine a lovely voice.* Your "leaning" comes from His heart of love.

The 1981 film *Chariots of Fire* features Scottish Olympic runner Eric Liddell. Before the 1924 games, he confirmed to his sister that he'd decided to go to China as a missionary but that first he needed to run. He told her how he believed God had made him for a purpose— for China, yes. But he also knew God had made him fast; he felt His pleasure when he ran. In using God's gift, Liddell hoped to win so that he could honor Him.

God made Eric Liddell fast. How has God made you? Musical? Analytical? Expressive with pen or voice? When we embrace our giftedness, we will feel His pleasure and bring honor to our Lord.

*Thank You, Father, for the joy of feeling Your pleasure
when we use Your gifts to us. Amen. —J.M.*

Truth That Transforms

Do not conform to the pattern of this world, but be transformed by the renewing of your mind. Then you will be able to test and approve what God's will is—his good, pleasing and perfect will.

ROMANS 12:2

Conformity plays a role in our lives from fashion and hairstyles to our home decor and dinner menus. Think about how you can often identify an era in photos by those clues. The "Throwback Thursday" pictures posted on Facebook often generate comments such as "Gotta love that '80s hairdo!"

Of course, the conformity the apostle Paul writes about in Romans 12 refers to behavior that runs deeper than our choices in the latest food and fashion crazes. We are to be distinct from the world, distinguished by our godly beliefs, actions, and attitudes. It takes courage to swim against the current of a culture that is not only opposed to biblical truths and values but also mocks them.

So how do we do that? By the truth that follows the "but" in Romans 12:2: "Be transformed." How? By the renewing of our minds, the ongoing process that happens when we begin each day with God in His Word and prayer. When we immerse ourselves daily in truth—in Jesus, who is Truth—the transformation within us will transfer to every aspect of our lives: belief, behavior, and the seeking of God's will.

Lord, thank You that we can live transformed
because of You, our Truth. Amen. —J.M.

Act Your Age?

Moses was one hundred and twenty years old when he died.
His eyes were not dim nor his natural vigor diminished.
DEUTERONOMY 34:7 NKJV

We've all heard the admonishment "Act your age." Plastered all over the internet on everything from T-shirts to towels is this response: "I don't know how to act my age. I've never been this old before." While that makes us smile, it also gives us something to think about. How *are* we to act in every age and stage in life?

So much is our mind-set, isn't it? Aging happens to all of us—with birthdays that come in a blink, it seems. Do you look in the mirror and think, *These wrinkles belong to my grandma. I don't feel old, so surely they can't be mine!*

A woman penned her prayerful thoughts on this topic:

"My identity is not in my age, it is in *Christ.* My identity isn't in anything that will *limit* me—it is in the limitless God who desires to do for me the impossible. My identity—who I am and what I am capable of—is in Christ alone. Thus, I can have utter confidence in my Creator, who knows exactly His good plans for me. Out of my confidence in my faithful God I can *rest* in Him. He will accomplish His best purposes for me."

Lord, thank You that our identity and our
confidence are found only in You. Amen. —J.M.

Our God-Breathed Bible

All Scripture is God-breathed and is useful for teaching,
rebuking, correcting and training in righteousness.
2 Timothy 3:16

Time to take inventory. How many Bibles do you own? How many different translations? By far, the Bible is the bestselling book of all time, with over one hundred million sold every year, or fifty Bibles sold every minute. Amazing, right?

Because of our easy access to the Bible, we regrettably take it for granted. In today's hectic homes, too often our Bibles collect dust instead of captivated readers. But when we learn about John Wycliffe and William Tyndale, early translators of the Bible into English, we are sobered. They suffered much while seeking to bring God's words of life to all.

Over the centuries, accounts have been told of the undeniable power of the inspired Word of God. Today those stories continue. The Gideon Bibles distributed in motels have not only changed lives but also, thankfully, saved many lives of those intending to commit suicide in that very motel. Instead they encountered Jesus through His Word.

Today, members of the persecuted Church around the world revere the Bible, especially converted Muslims who have discovered the powerful difference found in the *living* Word. They've been freed by every needed answer tucked between its covers. No other book on earth compares.

Let's enjoy the truth and treasures awaiting us in our Bibles today!

Lord, thank You for the life-changing
power found in Your Word. Amen. —J.M.

A Mother's Instinct

"As a mother comforts her child, so will I comfort you;
and you will be comforted over Jerusalem."
ISAIAH 66:13

When we are thrust into new roles, new seasons of our lives, we can often be consumed by a lack of confidence. In her role as a new mom, Rita was terrified when her first child was an infant, feeling clueless how to care for this helpless one who couldn't communicate with her.

Patty recalls the visit to her in-laws when her firstborn was five months old. Her mother-in-law, a mom of six, said and did things that made Patty question her ability to be a good mom. Years later she realized her sensitivity was due to her insecurities. Now that Patty has young grandkids of her own, she is extra careful to support their moms, which often means silence with a smile.

Megan knew her son, barely one, was sicker than a normal cold would warrant. His lethargy and lack of appetite concerned her, but two visits to the doctor made her feel like an overprotective mom. Days later, a chest X-ray, taken for something unrelated, revealed that her son had a serious case of pneumonia. The doctor apologized profusely, and Megan learned to listen to her maternal instinct.

You provide in every way, God, for every
role You give us. Thank You! Amen. —J.M.

A Table for One

The number of singles in our society has increased dramatically, with the numbers stretching beyond 50 percent for unmarried women. People living alone in 2016 reached beyond 28 percent. In spite of those higher numbers, we still live in a culture geared to couples.

Lisa remembers the first time after her divorce when she walked into a restaurant to dine alone. The young hostess, menus in hand, bent side to side to make sure no one was hiding behind Lisa's slender frame. Her question of "Only one?" ended on a high note of incredulity. When she gave Lisa the option of a single seat at the long bar flanked by the tables, Lisa nodded, just wanting to disappear—and quick! Grateful to have the table diners at her back, she watched the World Series on the screens above her.

Years later when Lisa returned to that coastal community for another getaway, she was prepared. When she entered the same eatery, book in hand, she responded to the same "Only one?" question with smiling affirmation. She chose a table surrounded by chatting diners and enjoyed her clam chowder in the company of a good read. Over the years she had submitted her singleness to God and gratefully learned that both her identity and confidence are found in Him.

Whatever our season, Lord, we are grateful for
the care and confidence You give. Amen. —J.M.

Most Assuredly

"Most assuredly, I say to you, he who
believes in Me has everlasting life."

JOHN 6:47 NKJV

When we wanted to convince a childhood friend of our promise to keep a secret, we maybe said the idiom "Cross my heart and hope to die, stick a needle in my eye," while finger-crossing our hearts. Or how about giving a "pinky promise" by interlocking your pinky with your friend's? Both were meant to add weight to our words.

In the book of John we find the term *most assuredly* twenty-five times and always spoken by Jesus. Bible translations often use "verily, verily," and "truly, truly." Some combine the two with "very truly," while the literal translation from the Greek is "amen, amen."

We normally use the word *amen* to end a prayer to express our agreement. It actually means "it is so" or "so it be." The word originates from the Hebrew, meaning "certainty" and "truth." So when Jesus said "most assuredly," we need to pay attention to what he's emphasizing!

Three times in John 3, Jesus used those words when speaking one night with Nicodemus, a ruler of the Jews, beginning with "Most assuredly, I say to you, unless one is born again, he cannot see the kingdom of God" (John 3:3 NKJV). Believing those words of Jesus and acting on them is the rock-solid basis of our faith and confidence in Christ. Have you been born again?

Jesus, thank You for Your gift of eternal life. Amen. —J.M.

Our Joy of Living

*Restore to me the joy of Your salvation,
and uphold me by Your generous Spirit.*
PSALM 51:12 NKJV

The employee at the box store exuded joy, and Diane immediately suspected one thing: *He's a Christian.* His friendliness and big smile gave away his close walk with Jesus, and one couldn't help but want to be around such warm cheer. She chatted with Chauncey in the check-out line and commented on his unusual name but had little time to say much else. Visiting from out of town, she wasn't sure she'd be back before her vacation ended.

Imagine her delight when she returned and found a beaming Chauncey at the front entrance. He was just changing duties, giving her time for a quick question. "What church do you go to?" His answer was immediate, and she beamed back at him. "I knew it! I knew you had to be a believer. You just radiate the love and joy of Jesus." The delightful conversation that ensued brought smiles to both their faces.

Do our lives show what Jesus has done for us? Or have the difficulties of life chiseled and chipped away at the bedrock of our joyful salvation? If our walk with our Lord looks like a funeral procession, let's pray that it becomes, instead, like the glad skipping of a beloved child.

*Jesus, as a song says, You truly are "the joy of living,"
and we pray to shine Your joy wherever we go. Amen. —J.M.*

God's Timings

*He has made everything beautiful in its time. He has also
set eternity in the human heart; yet no one can fathom
what God has done from beginning to end.*

ECCLESIASTES 3:11

Libby underlined 2 Peter 3:8 in her Bible: "But do not forget this one thing, dear friends: With the Lord a day is like a thousand years, and a thousand years are like a day." She couldn't resist penciling a smiley face in the margin along with the words "No kidding!"

Perhaps you can relate? Have you been waiting on an answer to prayer *forever*? Maybe it's the return of a prodigal child to his heavenly Father's arms—and to yours. Maybe it's your heart's yearning: a home, a spouse, or a child. Maybe you're praying for healing for you or for someone you love.

Waiting on heartfelt desires is downright difficult. Yet, the best part is how that waiting can draw us closer to the heart of God. In moving closer we hear His heartbeat of love and His voice of care and guidance. Human as we are, if we had no needs in our lives, we'd be apt to spend our time anywhere but with our Lord.

*Lord, while we often can't fathom Your ways and timings, we can
say with David, "But I trust in you, LORD; I say, 'You are my God.'
My times are in your hands" (Psalm 31:14–15). Amen. —J.M.*

No Green Thumb Required

But grow in the grace and knowledge of our Lord and Savior Jesus Christ. To him be glory both now and forever! Amen.

2 PETER 3:18

Since Melissa's large bedroom window was visible to her neighbor's driveway, she yearned for privacy. Her solution? A wall of ivy. Her mother warned her about the invasiveness of ivy, and Melissa laughed and agreed. "That's exactly why I want it, Mom."

She planted two small plants, and years later she loves her lush wall of green. Since the ivy also serves as the backdrop for a garden space framed by river rocks, it not only protects from prying eyes but also lifts her spirits. Yes, she has to trim back the ivy occasionally, but she's been grateful for its propensity to grow.

Anything alive will either grow or die. Nothing living remains the same. We determine what will grow in our gardens and also in our lives. We will grow either more loving or more indifferent. We'll nip bitterness in the bud, or we'll allow its pervasive roots to grow and send out offshoots of resentment and anger. We can also choose to grow in confidence with each new choice of courage.

Whether you're experiencing a growth spurt or dormancy right now, what do you wish to see flourish in the garden of your life today? Water with prayer, and see what God will do!

Above all, Lord, we want to grow more like You. Amen. —J.M.

This Same God

*And this same God who takes care of me will supply all your needs
from his glorious riches, which have been given to us in Christ Jesus.*
PHILIPPIANS 4:19 NLT

The apostle Paul ended his letter to the church at Philippi by recounting God's provisions, telling them he was "amply supplied" (v. 18 NIV) because of their gifts to him. But he didn't stop there; he reminded them that God would also meet *their* needs.

The words from various translations add oomph to Paul's beginning words: Know this, moreover, I am convinced. Are you convinced with Paul? Have you seen God come through in a crunch? Accounts of God's provisions fuel our faith and encourage us in our own times of need.

A single woman in her fifties received a check in the mail, arriving unexpectedly on Valentine's Day. She gasped when she saw the amount: $1,000! Her benefactor refused to let her return it, telling her that it was given in joyful obedience to God, to support her as a "missionary" in the community where she lived. That generous "love gift" enabled her to pay for some pressing needs.

You may be tempted to think those kinds of things don't or won't happen for you. But look again at the verse: "And this same God. . ." Yes! This same God, the One who provided for Paul, the single woman, and countless others will also provide for you.

Thank You, God, for Your timely provisions. Amen. —J.M.

A Lavish Love

"God loves you." You've probably heard those words plentiful times, but have you embraced the extent of His love for you? A lifetime won't be long enough to plumb the ocean depths of God's lavish love for us.

While decorating for Christmas one year, Jolene changed some decor in her living room, which left a big blank spot above her fireplace mantel. After some thought, she envisioned there a large oval mirror framed in gold. Every time she saw the bare space, she found herself saying aloud, "Thank You, God, for the mirror You're going to bring me."

When a friend came over to exchange gifts, she admired the festive Christmas decorations. Jolene mentioned the changes she had made and her prayer for the mirror she had in mind. Eyes dancing, her friend smiled. "I have a mirror like you described in my truck right now to take to the antiques store. It's yours if you want it." Sure enough, the mirror was exactly what Jolene had envisioned, and to this day she can't see it without sensing God's smile.

*Father, Your love for us is so amazing and sweet!
Thank You! Amen. —J.M.*

The Sound of Silence

*The fruit of that righteousness will be peace; its effect
will be quietness and confidence forever.*

Isaiah 32:17

Blaring horns, deafening music, wailing sirens, crying babies, barking dogs, rumbling trains, endless TV, radio, and internet videos. . .the list could go on and on. The proof is sound (no pun intended!) that we live in a noisy world. Sounds invade our every space—our homes, cars, our walks and workouts with podcasts and music, restaurants and stores, and even our church sanctuaries.

We've become so accustomed to noise that we no longer hear it. When Janna visited her friend in the next state, she was exhausted from her long drive. In the middle of the night, a roar awoke her out of a deep sleep and threw her into a momentary panic. *What was that?!* After her heart quit pounding, she realized it was a train. Her friend, accustomed to the rumble, slept right through it.

When's the last time you've sat in total silence? Can you be alone without some kind of sound-making device? Can you embrace silence in a conversation and be comfortable without having to immediately add your voice? Rare today is silence or the solitude that often accompanies it. In sweet silence is when we can best hear the heart whispers of God.

*Silence is Your gift to us, God. Help us to seek it so that
we can better hear You and Your wisdom. Amen. —J.M.*

God of Wonders

Who among the gods is like you, LORD? Who is like you—
majestic in holiness, awesome in glory, working wonders?
EXODUS 15:11

Mary loves to begin her mornings by reading her Bible and devotional books, and then she slips to her knees in prayer. In that time of quiet she enjoys praising God and also petitions Him with timely requests.

One morning her sister first came to mind, and as she began to pray for her upcoming marriage, every particular of her sister's situation came to mind in quick sequence. Mary mentally lifted it all up to God with the unexpected words that came out of her mouth, "Work Your wonders, Lord."

She prayed for a friend struggling in her marriage, seeing again in her mind's eye the specifics, like the three children, and the words came again, "Work Your wonders, Lord."

Her longtime friend, Kathy, faced a medical procedure the next day to try to get a prognosis on her health, and Mary lifted up her friend to God's care and prayed, "Work Your wonders, Lord."

She continued to do that with each person God brought to mind. "Work Your wonders, Lord." Mary's heart soared as she lifted each concern to her powerful God, confident that He would, indeed, work His wonders.

Lord, thank You for being our God who is "majestic in holiness"
and "awesome in glory." Work Your wonders, Lord. Amen. —J.M.

Open Hands

*"But who am I, and who are my people, that we should be able
to give as generously as this? Everything comes from you,
and we have given you only what comes from your hand."*
1 Chronicles 29:14

Give yourself a blessing and read 1 Chronicles 29 to enjoy King David's
exuberant prayer of praise. The king had gathered "the whole assembly" to report on the preparations for the temple that his son, Solomon,
would build. And then he gave the clarion call. "Now, who is willing to
consecrate themselves to the Lord today?" (1 Chronicles 29:5).

How King David's heart must have swelled in gratitude to God when
he saw all those in leadership respond with generous gifts from gold
to precious stones. Verse 9 tells us, "The people rejoiced at the willing
response of their leaders, for they had given freely and wholeheartedly
to the Lord."

Since everything on heaven and earth is God's, we also can
be generous with everything God gives to us. Out of what is His—
greatness, power, glory, majesty, and splendor—He blesses us so we
can bless others. That's key to remember. What He places in our hands
isn't meant to be hoarded but to be willingly shared with others. After
all, how can He give us more if our fingers are clasped tightly around
what we already have?

*Lord, help us to keep open hands so we can freely
pass on what You've given. Amen. —J.M.*

Look Inside

But the L ORD said to Samuel, "Do not consider his appearance or his height, for I have rejected him. The L ORD does not look at the things people look at. People look at the outward appearance, but the L ORD looks at the heart."

1 S AMUEL 16:7

You know the old saying "Don't judge a book by its cover," and how that adage is often applied to people: don't judge others based on their appearance. Yet how prone we are to do that! In fact, it's been proved over and over how we make snap judgments—in one to seven seconds—when we first meet someone.

In our culture that caters to youth and beauty, little room is left for the average or marginalized person. What is your bias? What comes to mind when you see people who fit these descriptions: obese, tattooed, white-haired, in a wheelchair, multiple face and body piercings, turban on head, purple hair. Did your thoughts surprise you?

We've all heard stories of children ignoring a person's outside and seeing the inside—who the person truly is. Let's follow their example and see beyond the exterior. Thankfully, that's what God does with each one of us. He goes beyond the visible to view our hearts.

Thank You, Lord, for looking at our hearts with love, and help us to do the same for one another. Amen. —J.M.

A Winsome Witness

Be wise in the way you act toward outsiders; make the most of
every opportunity. Let your conversation be always full of grace,
seasoned with salt, so that you may know how to answer everyone.
COLOSSIANS 4:5–6

Say the word *witness* to Christians, and watch them cringe with discomfort. While we desire for others to know Jesus, most of us feel guilty because we do so little to fulfill that desire. We can recite the reasons why: we don't know the Bible well enough to answer their questions; we're too fearful to even try.

What if we so enjoyed living our lives with Jesus that people can't help but ask what is different about us? Walking our talk in a winsome way attracts people to us. When we show the love and compassion of Jesus in our conversations, really listening to others' concerns, God is likely to swing open the door for more in-depth conversations.

When we know and love God deeply, we can't help but echo Peter and John in Acts 4:20: "As for us, we cannot help speaking about what we have seen and heard." And just as salt makes food more palatable, when our words are seasoned with kindness and caring, they can be received as tasty morsels of truth.

Lord, give us such a love for others that they will long to know You.
Help us to be winsome to win some to You. Amen. —J.M.

Mentoring Moms

Likewise, teach the older women to be reverent in the way they live, not to be slanderers or addicted to much wine, but to teach what is good. Then they can urge the younger women to love their husbands and children.

TITUS 2:3–4

The word *mentor* dates back to the 1600s, but it's become a more familiar term in recent years. Usually the goal of a mentor is to help another navigate the current seas of her life, which in today's world often means the upheaval that comes with motherhood.

Paul's words to older women in the book of Titus on how to live and teach younger women have birthed the phrase "a Titus 2 woman" within the church. You may already have such a relationship in your life that happened in an organic way. If so, be grateful, since the mentoring relationship is most successful when there is a natural rapport between two women.

If you're older, perhaps God has placed a young mom in your life, and you'd like to pour into her what you found helpful during your mothering years. Learning from your failings and tips that saved your sanity could move her from the need-to-survive to glad-to-thrive mode. Or you may be the young mom eyeing that mature woman you'd like to emulate. Reach out, and see what good things God has in mind for both of you.

Bring together, dear Lord, sweet and helpful relationships ordained by You. —J.M.

Friends from Afar

*One generation commends your works to another; they tell
of your mighty acts. They speak of the glorious splendor of
your majesty—and I will meditate on your wonderful works.
They tell of the power of your awesome works—and I will
proclaim your great deeds. They celebrate your abundant
goodness and joyfully sing of your righteousness.*

PSALM 145:4–7

Mentoring friendships are God's wonderful gifts to us as women, but sometimes geography and circumstances require us to seek support elsewhere. Many women find online groups helpful, especially when going through a deep sorrow like pregnancy loss. The community of other mourning moms can offer understanding like no one else.

Encouragement, solace, and understanding can also be found in quality Christian books. Authors can mentor us from afar—and even from the past. While there's an array of excellent choices today, also consider these writers' works or their biographies for inspiration and guidance: Elisabeth Elliot, Edith Schaeffer, Catherine Marshall, Eugenia Price, Amy Carmichael, Corrie ten Boom, and Ruth Bell Graham.

Today's women would benefit from the gems contained in *The Hidden Art of Homemaking* by Edith Schaeffer or *Stepping Heavenward* by Elizabeth Prentiss. We can find kindred spirits in authors, their fictional characters, or in hymn writers like Fanny Crosby, blinded as an infant, and Frances Ridley Havergal, a lovely soul from England. Enjoy making some new friends from afar, yet close in heart.

*Thank You for the rich legacy these
lives have left us, Lord. Amen. —J.M.*

No Rocking Chairs Allowed!

*They will still bear fruit in old age, they will stay
fresh and green, proclaiming, "The LORD is upright;
he is my Rock, and there is no wickedness in him."*

PSALM 92:14–15

Friends of all ages enrich our lives and add joy to our journeys, don't
they? Kitty is one of those friends to Lana. They met many years ago
and recently reconnected online. Although Kitty is now eighty-three,
she is still proclaiming who Jesus is with great joy.

Readers of her books have contacted her from around the world,
including a young man in India and a Muslim husband and father in the
Middle East. Kitty spends many hours crafting emails to answer their
questions about Jesus. She also sends out email updates to friends who
pray for those men and other seekers.

Her life as a speaker is one of the ways Kitty is still bearing "fruit in
old age" and staying "fresh and green." She'll soon speak four times
during a week in Oregon, followed by two weeks in Wisconsin, where
she'll speak seven times. She wrote Lana, "Next week I'll be involved
as an actor in a police training film. . .and so it goes. Death is going to
have to run me down! I'm not going to sit and wait for it! And, oh, BTW,
I plan to go zip-lining while in Oregon and am soooo excited!"

Lord, can I please be like Kitty when I grow up? Amen. —J.M.

Stargazing

God made two great lights—the greater light to govern the day and the lesser light to govern the night. He also made the stars.

GENESIS 1:16

For a night of celestial delight, mark your calendar to see the Perseid meteor shower in mid-August. Research online to learn the optimum night and conditions, and then sit back to enjoy a star-spangled display of God's creation. Normal years yield sixty to seventy meteors per hour, but an outburst year like 2016 offered 150-200 per hour. You may want to memorize Psalm 8 beforehand, so its words can sing in your heart while you watch the heavenly bling:

> LORD, our Lord, how majestic is your name in all the earth! You have set your glory in the heavens. . . . When I consider your heavens, the work of your fingers, the moon and the stars, which you have set in place, what is mankind that you are mindful of them, human beings that you care for them?
> (Psalm 8:1, 3–4)

God's "glory in the heavens" includes ten billion galaxies in our observable universe. With an average of one hundred billion stars per galaxy, that takes the total to one billion trillion—that's twenty-one zeros following the one! Those numbers are even more impressive in light of Psalm 147:4: "He determines the number of the stars and calls them each by name." Wow.

We're amazed by You, God, and grateful that You know the stars—and us—by name. Amen. —J.M.

Battle Weary?

"This is what the LORD says to you: 'Do not be afraid or discouraged because of this vast army. For the battle is not yours, but God's.' "
2 CHRONICLES 20:15

What "vast army" is facing you today? What "battle" is badgering you, causing you to wring your hands in despair? Take hope, friend, and take heart at God's encouragement to all of us: this battle isn't ours but God's!

When King Jehoshaphat learned that a vast army was coming against him, he was understandably alarmed. But he "resolved to inquire of the LORD" (2 Chronicles 20:3) and did so before all the people, ending with, "We do not know what to do, but our eyes are on you" (v. 12).

We often don't know what to do either, do we? But we can follow what the Spirit of the Lord said through Jahaziel, when he proclaimed that the battle was not theirs but God's. He spoke more encouraging words as an excellent example to us today: You will not have to fight this battle. Stand firm, and see the deliverance the Lord will give you. Do not be afraid; do not be discouraged. The Lord will be with you. Have faith in the Lord your God and you will be upheld (v. 17).

The best thing? They began to sing, "Give thanks to the LORD, for his love endures forever" (v. 21). And as they sang and praised, "the LORD set ambushes" (v. 22)—and that was that!

God, You astonish us! Thank You for fighting our battles as only You can. Amen. —J.M.

This Walk of Faith

So we are always confident, knowing that while we are at home in the body we are absent from the Lord. For we walk by faith, not by sight. We are confident, yes, well pleased rather to be absent from the body and to be present with the Lord.

2 Corinthians 5:6–8 NKJV

Are you a planner? You know, the kind who makes all the arrangements for a trip ahead of time, with a detailed daily itinerary? If so, the more spontaneous traveler may try your patience!

Those traits show up in novelists too, with the planning writer, "the plotter," outlining the entire book before beginning. Her counterpart, "the pantser," the one who writes "by the seat of her pants," will know her story idea and characters and *maybe* how the story ends but has no idea how it will all come about.

Our differing personalities make it more difficult for some to "walk by faith, not by sight." The planners prefer to map out their lives, so they can systematically go toward their destination. But whether a plotter or pantser, detours and delays frustrate all of life's travelers. At times we may even question if the hard journey is worth it. Take heart, friends, and focus on Jesus and the joys that await us. Every step of this walk by faith will be more than worthwhile when we behold our heavenly home and see our Savior's face.

To someday see Your face, Jesus—what joy! Amen. —J.M.

The Cactus Wren

Stand firm then, with the belt of truth buckled around your waist, with the breastplate of righteousness in place, and with your feet fitted with the readiness that comes from the gospel of peace. In addition to all this, take up the shield of faith, with which you can extinguish all the flaming arrows of the evil one. Take the helmet of salvation and the sword of the Spirit, which is the word of God.

EPHESIANS 6:14–17

One could easily say that the cactus wren is full of courage. This little birdie can navigate through quite a labyrinth of razor-sharp spines to make its home in a cactus. Why? To protect itself from predators.

Like the wren, we too must protect ourselves from predators—only the spiritual kind, like Satan. In order to navigate this fallen earth and to escape the piercing effects of sin, we need to have the confidence that we can prevail. So as followers of Christ, how can we truly be courageous and triumphant in a world that is determined to destroy our faith, our witness, and our hope? This passage in Ephesians is the answer to that age-old question. It's a powerful passage for us to memorize or tape to the bathroom mirror!

Lord, please help me to fulfill what You've ask me to do in Your Word, so that I might stay spiritually strong! Amen. —A.H.

Love Changes Everything

But now, this is what the LORD says—
he who created you, Jacob,
he who formed you, Israel:
"Do not fear, for I have redeemed you;
I have summoned you by name; you are mine."

ISAIAH 43:1

Falling in love can be pure bliss. And one of the things couples like to do to declare that love is to carve their names in a tree. They might even add two interconnected hearts just to highlight their affection—two hearts as one.

Hard to comprehend, but the Lord cares for us even more profoundly than the most ardently devoted suitor or the most protective, devoted mother. The book of Isaiah says that He has summoned you by name. He says, "You are mine." Oh, to be cherished so deeply!

God loves us—enough to make the ultimate sacrifice—and that love changes everything. The way we perceive ourselves. The way we get up in the morning. The way we talk with confidence to people. Our purpose and the choices we make. Our redemption, our aging process, and our eternity. Yes, His love changes everything, and it was God who invented such a marvelous emotion. Have you thanked Him today for such an extraordinary blessing?

Lord, I'm so happy You invented love. It is a beautiful
thing to behold! And thank You for loving me so greatly.
Help me to reflect that love in all I do. Amen. —A.H.

Frivolous or Ferocious?

Jesus said to him, "[You say to Me,] 'If You can?' All things are possible for the one who believes and trusts [in Me]!" Immediately the father of the boy cried out [with a desperate, piercing cry], saying, "I do believe; help [me overcome] my unbelief."
MARK 9:23–24 AMP

Interesting thing about faith—when things are moving along fairly well, it is easy to feel we wield a big, bold faith. The kind that can make the clouds part and the mountains tremble. But what happens when bad stuff happens? When you watch as your best friend lives the dream you had always longed for? Or when the doctor gives you or your loved one the gravest of news? Or when your grown daughter says she not only has left the Christian faith but also is now moving far away from you? What then?

God will still be there even when our faith falters. Even when we feel we can no longer move a molehill, let alone a mountain. Ask the Lord to replace your frivolous faith for a ferocious one. Cry out as the man did to Jesus, "I do believe; help me overcome my unbelief."

Lord, sometimes I have no more than a mustard seed of faith, but I am confident You can grow that small kernel into a mighty tree! Amen. —A.H.

A New Wolf in Town

*And what do you benefit if you gain the whole world but
lose your own soul? Is anything worth more than your soul?*

MARK 8:36–37 NLT

There is a new wolf in sheep's clothing, and this New Age creature
promises us that if we ask the forces of the cosmos for anything, we'll
get it. If you want cash, fame, a big house, a fancy car, all you need to
do is put in your request. You need to believe, of course, but then you
just wait for the goodies to roll in. This concept would be ridiculous if
it weren't so dangerous.

Why? Because it romances the notion that we can be in control of
our own destiny. We can do better than God. We can have whatever
pleasures we want—right now.

Even if we could somehow make this concept work, why would we
wish for anything that God wouldn't want for us? What if our demands
could cause us harm or cause us to lose our very soul? As it says in
Mark, "Is anything worth more than your soul?" Even though God does
give us good gifts and even though the Bible tells us that God wants to
give us our hearts' desires, Christ's prayer before His crucifixion says it
all when He added, "Not my will, but thine, be done" (Luke 22:42 KJV).

*Holy Spirit, please give me Your confident, exhorting,
and loving words of truth to help people flee
from Satan's enticements. Amen. —A.H.*

His Divine Music

It is he who made the earth by his power,
who established the world by his wisdom,
and by his understanding stretched out the heavens.
JEREMIAH 10:12 ESV

Don't you just love music? It has the power to soothe, invigorate, refresh, and inspire. God must love music too because He not only rouses and stirs humanity to create it, but also fills nature with a kind of music. Think of the enormous variety of birds that sing to us. The coyotes with their baying echo through the canyons. The wind that whistles, the brooks that burble, and the zephyrs that sigh through the willows. The thunder that drums and the seas that crash like cymbals. Nature's music brings us pleasure and joy and it glorifies God—the One who created it with His mighty power.

Perhaps when you feel life is whirling out of control, take a walk in nature and enjoy the Lord's fashioned splendor and His orchestra of divine music. He made you a beautiful garden called Earth. Go tend it. Go enjoy it in the cool of the evening. Let it bring you confidence—that the One who not only holds all of nature in His hand also holds you.

I love all that You have created, Lord. Thank You for Your beautiful
music and how it refreshes me for another day! Amen. —A.H.

The Desire to Be a Hero

How great is our Lord! His power is absolute!
His understanding is beyond comprehension!
PSALM 147:5 NLT

Confused and upset, the woman you see roaming the busy street is lost. She admits she has Alzheimer's, and you discover that she's gotten separated from her sister. You assure the woman that you will not leave her until you find her sister. And you keep your word. You set aside your plans for the day to make sure all goes well. When you finally bring about the reunion of the two sisters, they rejoice and your heart sings.

Christ is the greatest hero of all time—"Great is our Lord! His power is absolute! His understanding is beyond comprehension!" And Job says, "These are just the beginning of all that he does, merely a whisper of his power. Who, then, can comprehend the thunder of his power?" (Job 26:14 NLT). Because we are made in the Lord's image, we too desire to be a hero. We feel such joy emulating Him and reflecting His tender care that it brings us a lightness of being. And it makes God smile too.

Whose hero will you be today?

Lord, I want to do good works because I'm grateful
to You for all that You've done for me—for being
the ultimate hero of my life! Amen. —A.H.

What Makes Us Beautiful

Charm is deceptive, and beauty does not last;
but a woman who fears the Lord will be greatly praised.
PROVERBS 31:30 NLT

The young woman at the party seems to sparkle all over the place, even more than her shimmery cheek powder and her rhinestone jewelry. She is giddy with charms, effervescent with a dewy youthfulness, and gifted with a classical chiseled beauty. And it's taking every pore of your Christianity not to take an immediate dislike to her!

Reason? Most women would like to be beautiful and charming and admired by the masses. Some of this desire comes from envying—only slightly, of course—overly airbrushed models on magazine covers and ultra-polished celebrities fluttering hither and thither like pretty butterflies. Nothing wrong with wanting to look our best; however, too many times our confidence as women hangs too heavily on the way we look. If we are too consumed by our reflection in the mirror, we won't have enough time and vitality and creative energy left to do all that God has gifted us and called us to do! There's the rub.

May our confidence as women never rely on the world's opinions but always rest in the way Christ sees us, loves us. And may we know that reverence for the Lord is not only wise, but it makes us beautiful and worthy of praise!

Lord, may I wake up every morning knowing You see
me as Your beautiful and beloved one. Amen. —A.H.

Only the Beginning

For to us a child is born, to us a son is given, and the government will be on his shoulders. And he will be called Wonderful Counselor, Mighty God, Everlasting Father, Prince of Peace.

ISAIAH 9:6

Christmas is a spectacular holiday of hope and beauty. Who doesn't love all the fragrant boughs of greenery, the warm wishes, the caroling on a snowy night, the spicy wassail, and the holy hush of a candlelight service? But most of all, there is that baby in the manger. So sweet and tender is the scene with Jesus and His mother, Mary, that we sigh all the way down to our souls. We might even be tempted to leave the infant in the manger, since we can relate more to a cooing baby than to the commanding presence of a mighty, risen Savior.

Thank the good Lord that Christmas is not the end of the story but only the beginning. We who are frail and fallen sinners need not only the heart tugs of the gentle manger scene but also the power of Easter morning and that glorious empty tomb. This, yes, this is the rest of the story for all humanity. Rejoice!

Lord, may I always carry Christmas in my heart, and may I never hesitate to share the glorious news of Easter morning! Amen. —A.H.

Pulling Out All the Stops

*He answered, " 'Love the Lord your God with all your heart
and with all your soul and with all your strength and with
all your mind'; and, 'Love your neighbor as yourself.' "*

LUKE 10:27

People love rooting for their favorite sports team. They go all out with the right T-shirt, hat, and the best seats in the stadium. People have a passion for their hobbies and pleasures and vacations. Spare no expense. Sometimes we even do it up big when it comes to sin. Uh-oh. Not so cool. When it comes to God, do we choose to pull out all the stops? Okay, so how can we do that?

Do you love God with all your heart, soul, strength, and mind? Do you have a passion for God's Living Word? Do you trust the Lord extravagantly and shun sin? Do you praise Him as fervently as you cheer on your favorite team? Do you go big when it comes to offering a portion of your time and talent to the needy, to good causes, and to the church?

God gives us many kinds of things to do in this life, and He wants to bring us joy. But do we in turn bring joy to God in the way we live?

*Lord, show me where I need to improve when it comes
to using my time, talent, and treasures. Amen. —A.H.*

Confidence in a World Unseen

For we walk by faith, not by sight [living our lives in a manner
consistent with our confident belief in God's promises].

2 CORINTHIANS 5:7 AMP

We live in a world that we perceive through our senses, and all of that sensory detail is an important and intricate part of our daily reality. It allows us to maneuver through this life with some measure of confidence. But sometimes we come to trust this physical world so profoundly that the idea of an invisible realm seems fantastical.

And yet the Word of God tells us to walk by faith not by sight, a notion we are not entirely comfortable with. So how does one live by faith then? How does one have confidence in a world that is predominantly unseen to us in this earthly kingdom?

A follower of Christ might say, "Daily, Lord, I enjoy Your creation. Your glorious handiwork. I feel Your presence, Your stirring hand, ever guiding me, helping me along my way. I have benefited from Your salvation, Your gifts, Your miracles, and the divine love You continue to pour into my life. I accept all of these truths by faith, and I will continue to be confident in Your promises!"

Lord, I thank You for all the ways You make
Yourself known to me. I love You! Amen. —A.H.

When Sorrow Comes

*For the kind of sorrow God wants us to experience leads
us away from sin and results in salvation. There's no
regret for that kind of sorrow. But worldly sorrow,
which lacks repentance, results in spiritual death.*
2 CORINTHIANS 7:10 NLT

There is no getting around this truth—life can be a harsh landscape. At times, it's an almost unbearable road to walk. And there are many kinds of sorrow. Humankind knows them all by heart. The Word of God tells us that a worldly kind of sorrow, which springs from a lack of belief in Christ, well, that kind of grief is not just useless, but it produces death. Why? Because it is a dead tree trying to produce good fruit. But godly sorrow— the kind that is repentant and the kind God wants us to experience—will lead us away from sin and results in salvation, which holds no regret.

So when we feel despair creeping into our hearts, we should ask ourselves why our hearts are grieving. Is it from seeing life through worldly glasses?

*Dear God, when sorrow does come to me,
I pray that You will turn it into what is right and good
in Your sight. In Jesus' name I pray. Amen. —A.H.*

Angels Watching Over Us

For he will command his angels concerning
you to guard you in all your ways.
PSALM 91:11 ESV

It's a sweet notion, telling our kids at night about their guardian angel, but do we truly believe it? Or has this idea taken on a make-believe quality like the fairy tales we read them? The Bible makes it clear that there are many instances when God used and still uses His angels to interact with humans in a variety of ways. One might ask, "If we have angels guarding us, then why do we still have bad things happening to us?" It is a valid question with an answer that is anything but simple.

We live in a fallen world, and because of our sin, bad things do happen. God could stop anything, yes, and give us every request we make, but we—who are fallible with transgressions—cannot fully comprehend the divine ways of our Creator. We do know that God does not allow anything to happen to us that we cannot bear and that all things work for our good. We also know that there must be countless times when angels keep us safe from potential incidents of harm, physically as well as mentally and spiritually. We may never know the extent of an angel's intervention on our behalf, but what we can do is thank God for His help and mercy!

Lord, thank You for sending Your
angels to watch over me. Amen. —A.H.

That Life May Go Well

*But I gave them this command: Obey me, and I will be
your God and you will be my people. Walk in obedience
to all I command you, that it may go well with you.*

JEREMIAH 7:23

If you've ever been fortunate enough to attract bluebirds to nest in your backyard, you'll know how beautiful they are to watch. But if you place that special bluebird house too close to your own home, you'll soon discover they are territorial, and they will flutter and tap on your windows until you're either pulling your hair out or you're wanting to put up a FOR SALE sign on that birdhouse!

It doesn't take much in this life—one twist or two—and a joy like watching bluebirds can become a torment. So it goes with our spiritual lives. As long as we stay within God's precepts, our lives will know peace and joy. But if we allow ourselves to twist what is right and trade what is good for evil—and if we get off the path the Lord has set before us—well, there's going to be trouble. May we learn from past experiences, and may we continually grow in maturity and confidence in the Lord.

*Lord, show me how to walk in obedience,
that life may go well for me. Amen. —A.H.*

The "Feel-Good Gospel"

Two others, criminals, were led out to be executed with him at a place called "The Skull." There all three were crucified—Jesus on the center cross, and the two criminals on either side. "Father, forgive these people," Jesus said, "for they don't know what they are doing." And the soldiers gambled for his clothing, throwing dice for each piece.

LUKE 23:32–34 TLB

Haven't you heard? The good news of the Gospel is outdated. People don't want to hear it anymore. It's not convenient enough, pacifying enough, and politically correct enough. The words *salvation* and *repentance* no longer fit the new demographic. What reasonable person could ask anyone to give up sinning anyway? It's what gets us through a difficult life!

Maybe we need a more upbeat, progressive church that connects with the current culture? Why can't our worship music deify a music idol instead of the God of the Bible? Why can't the Gospel reflect our ever-changing sensibilities? Why can't we just close the doors of the church and dance in the streets? Why can't we rewrite the Bible and make it reflect our ever-changing beliefs, our pleasure-seeking gratifications, our freedom to do whatever makes us happy at the moment?

Why can't we be God? It's a tempting, modern concept, and yet it's as old as the Garden of Eden.

Lord God, forgive us as a community, a nation,
and a world. We know not what we do. Amen. —A.H.

The Gift of Compassion

Blessed be the God and Father of our Lord Jesus Christ, the Father of mercies and God of all comfort, who comforts us in all our affliction, so that we may be able to comfort those who are in any affliction, with the comfort with which we ourselves are comforted by God. For as we share abundantly in Christ's sufferings, so through Christ we share abundantly in comfort too.
2 Corinthians 1:3–5 esv

You are skipping along through life like a kid high on candy when suddenly you trip. On a curb. In the pouring rain. And then you land full force on your knee. Pain burns through you. You scream. Your knee balloons up purple. You moan. You pray. Tears run down your cheek.

For a season, you will have a close relationship with pain. You may not have mobility or your dignity. But the one thing you will have—if you allow it—is the power of empathy. You know now—if only for a little while—what it might feel like to deal with chronic pain or to need a cane, a walker, or a wheelchair. God has comforted us in all our afflictions, and we should bring comfort to others. Our empathy will help us to encourage those who suffer. Those who need what we have to offer—the gift of compassion.

Holy Spirit, show me the friend I can bring comfort to today. Amen. —A.H.

His Hand of Victory!

*"Do not fear [anything], for I am with you; do not be afraid,
for I am your God. I will strengthen you, be assured I will help
you; I will certainly take hold of you with My righteous right
hand [a hand of justice, of power, of victory, of salvation]."*

ISAIAH 41:10 AMP

You wake up in a pool of sweat. Yes, another nightmare has jolted you
from a sound sleep. Fears of all shapes and sizes creep in, and you
wonder how you will ever get back to sleep. The argument you had
with your daughter weighs on your mind. Your boss promoted someone
ahead of you—someone much less qualified. Your mother loves you,
but doesn't understand you. Then a whole host of "what ifs" begin their
usual torture routine. You wonder, "What if those sharp pains in my
head mean I have a brain tumor?" and "What if no one wants to care for
me in my old age?" or "I don't deserve God's mercy and grace. What
if He abandons me?"

Don't let the enemy of your soul torment you. Don't believe his lies.
Be instead confident in God's love for you, no matter the day or hour.
Do not be afraid. He will help you. His hand of justice, power, victory,
and salvation will take hold of you and give you strength!

*Thank You, Lord, that I need not fear this world because
You take hold of me with Your righteous hand. Amen. —A.H.*

Baby Food

For though by this time you ought to be teachers, you need someone to teach you again the basic principles of the oracles of God. You need milk, not solid food, for everyone who lives on milk is unskilled in the word of righteousness, since he is a child. But solid food is for the mature, for those who have their powers of discernment trained by constant practice to distinguish good from evil.
HEBREWS 5:12–14 ESV

A big jar of prune puree baby food. Wow, now that packs some memories, right? Good or bad. But even if you grew fond of the sweet brown goo as a child, you sure wouldn't want to live on it for a lifetime!

And yet isn't that what we do spiritually as Christians when we refuse to grow up in the Lord? When we don't seem to even know the basic precepts found in God's Word? Christians need to ask the Holy Spirit for wisdom and discernment. We need to stay close to God through prayer, reading His Word, and staying connected to a Bible-believing church. Then we will be able to live more righteously, distinguishing good from evil. This is vital, since all sorts of false teachings are not only seeping into our culture but are also brazenly storming through the doors of the church and sometimes even preaching from the pulpit!

Holy Spirit, teach me how to move from milk to solid food. Amen. —A.H.

The Sound of Her Own Voice

The one who has knowledge uses words with restraint,
and whoever has understanding is even-tempered.

PROVERBS 17:27

Have you ever met someone who loved—I mean loved—the sound of her own voice? It could be at a party, or at work, or even at church. Her talk might start out interesting, but there is just sooo much of it. Like a locomotive that has lost any use of its brakes. You eventually glaze over, and instead of hearing something logical coming out of her mouth, it morphs into "Waahhh, waahhh, waahhh. . ."

Proverbs says that if we have knowledge, we will use restraint in our words. Proverbs 13:3 (ESV) takes the caution even further by saying, "Whoever guards his mouth preserves his life; he who opens wide his lips comes to ruin." Okay, that is pretty heavy.

If we want to gain someone's confidence, then we need to think before we speak. And in some cases, pray before we speak. Let the other person have her say too. Ask questions and really listen rather than cooking up the next thing to say. That's the way to win friends, the way to open the door to witnessing about Christ, and the way to live well.

Lord, please help me to be a woman who
is wise with her words. Amen. —A.H.

Being Forgetful

Your heavenly Father will forgive you if you forgive those who sin against you; but if you refuse to forgive them, he will not forgive you.
MATTHEW 6:14–15 TLB

Forgetfulness is easy. Like what was that movie you saw a week ago? When was your friend's birthday? What was the name of that newcomer at church—the one who is waving at you and walking toward you right now?

But sometimes our memory is perfect, like when it comes to wrongs people have done to us. Boy, sometimes we can remember a misdeed with military precision—every meticulous detail right down to the smug curl of her lip and the curt tone of her voice. Sometimes we remember easily because we refuse to forgive. We just want to hold on to the hurt, thinking it's somehow our right, our revenge. But an unwillingness to forgive will only fester into bitterness and unhappiness.

We are reminded in the book of Matthew that if we are determined not to forgive, then God will not forgive us. Pretty clear. Pretty simple. But you're thinking, *Yes, but in my humanness, it is just not doable.* No, it isn't. But be assured that with God all things are possible, even forgiving those pesky offenses.

Lord, I admit it's hard to forgive some of the people who have wronged me. Show me how to forgive them and then become truly forgetful about those trespasses. Amen. —A.H.

The Author of Love

*Dear friends, let us practice loving each other, for love comes
from God and those who are loving and kind show that they
are the children of God, and that they are getting to know
him better. But if a person isn't loving and kind, it shows
that he doesn't know God—for God is love.*

1 JOHN 4:7–8 TLB

Don't you just love good and loyal friends—the ones who love you no
matter what?

Maybe you're at lunch with your gal-friend, and you feel comfortable to just be you. You show her not only the faith-filled facets of
your personality, but you allow her to see your frailties as a Christian.
That can be scary. Then you wonder, *Was I too real? Did I share too
much of me? What will she do?*

And then you sigh with calm assurance and sweet relief. Your friend
did not nitpick at you or criticize you. She didn't gift you back with a
perky sermon with a ribbon tied just so. She gave you kindness and
encouragement—and love. And where did she find that love? From
God, for He is the Author of love.

*God, thank You for friends who love me no matter what.
They are treasures, and they give me the confidence to
keep going. Please bless each of my friends today in
some special way. In Jesus' name I pray. Amen. —A.H.*

Praying with Confidence!

*The prayer of a righteous person has
great power as it is working.*

JAMES 5:16 ESV

When it comes to prayer, well, a thousand queries come to mind. And sometimes those questions stay and weigh heavily on our spirits. Such as, *Do I have enough faith to make this prayer work? Is God really listening? Do I need to kneel when I pray? Is my request too impossible or too insignificant? How many prayers will it take to move this mountain in my life? Do I need a whole prayer team on my side or is one fervent prayer from me enough?*

We can learn about prayer from Jesus' example. He would often go away to a quiet place to pray. Prayer was a vital part of His life. And Christ even gave us an example in His Word on how we can pray. In addition, in the book of James, we discover that there is great power in the prayer of a righteous person. That gives us confidence. We do not have to be perfect for our prayers to be effective, but we do need to be honorable and faithful to God. We do not need a great deal of faith but merely a mustard seed. God has made a miraculous way for us to talk with Him. How encouraging! Shall we begin?

*Lord, help me to never forget how
powerful my prayers are. Amen.* —A.H.

That Quiet Place

The LORD is my shepherd; I have all that I need. He lets me rest in green meadows; he leads me beside peaceful streams.
PSALM 23:1–2 NLT

You're on a hike, and even though your body is saying, "No more," you get that overpowering urge to conquer the trail. However, the day is a scorcher, you're getting low on water, and you are indeed beyond tired. You might even be lost! But no matter what happens, you want to finish the hike. Hmm. How many different ways can we say *foolish*?

Why do we always have to conquer everything in this life until we nearly drop from exhaustion? Until we've lost our focus and we become downright cranky? Instead of defeating the trail, you could let God use its wonder and beauty to capture your heart a little. You might hear the songbirds that you hadn't noticed before, or the silky breeze tickling your skin, or the chatty leaves, or the scent of deep woods and wildflowers. There in that quiet place, allow your soul to remember that the Lord is your Shepherd. You have all you need in Him. Shall we let Him lead us to those green pastures and those peaceful streams? To inspire us, refresh us, and to renew our confidence in Him?

I love the beauty of Your earth, Lord. Please show me when I should hike with gusto and when I should quiet myself before You. Amen. —A.H.

The Illusion of Invincibility

Yet you do not know what tomorrow will bring. What is your life? For you are a mist that appears for a little time and then vanishes. Instead you ought to say, "If the Lord wills, we will live and do this or that."

JAMES 4:14–15 ESV

When we are young, we think we will live forever. Or at least we feel safe enough that we can put off pondering death and eternity—for now. In reality, though, we don't know what tomorrow will bring with our health, our careers, our plans, our loved ones, or even our very lives.

But still, that intoxicating feeling of invincibility entices us because we want control. And yet human control is only smoke and mirrors. The sermons of self-reliance and empowerment that the world preaches do us great spiritual harm. Even if we find ourselves presiding over vast audiences with the charisma and power to sway them with our words like the wind waves the wheat, well, at the end of the day, we are still not God. Instead we are like a mist that appears for a little time and then vanishes. We are vulnerable, fragile, desperate creatures, fallen and broken, and in great need of a Savior. Even though that message isn't glamorous enough to make it on the popular talk shows, it is truth.

Lord, I know You alone are in control of my life,
and that is exactly how I want it to be! Amen. —A.H.

Whispers of Truth

"And the son said to him, 'Father, I have sinned against heaven and before you. I am no longer worthy to be called your son.' But the father said to his servants, 'Bring quickly the best robe, and put it on him, and put a ring on his hand, and shoes on his feet. And bring the fattened calf and kill it, and let us eat and celebrate. For this my son was dead, and is alive again; he was lost, and is found.' And they began to celebrate."

LUKE 15:21–24 ESV

You sink onto the couch with despair. You might binge-watch TV until you're ill. You might succumb to the temptation of gluttony or drink your way into a blur. Why? Because you think you're hopeless. You want to repent and run into the arms of Jesus, but you keep thinking, *I've gone too far. Sinned too much. Even God doesn't want me now.*

Well, don't you believe it. Read the whole story of the prodigal son in Luke, and you will be able to discern where your hopeless thoughts are coming from—the enemy. But here's the good news—God wants you back. Here are His whispers of truth, *"You are My daughter. I love you. Come home. We will celebrate, because My daughter was dead, and now she's alive!"*

Dearest Lord, I'm sorry for my sin. Thank You for Your forgiveness and for welcoming me back home! Amen. —A.H.

As Sweet as Heaven

But when the Holy Spirit controls our lives he will produce this kind of fruit in us: love, joy, peace, patience, kindness, goodness, faithfulness.
GALATIANS 5:22 TLB

If we aren't careful, we can become small-minded. You know, those cheap shots in a crowd to make us look better or smarter. Those little jabs to our spouse to prove we are right, no matter what kind of pain it might cause or what arguments it might raise. Those backhanded compliments to our coworkers and the offhanded words that stir up trouble rather than foster an atmosphere of peace. Or those cleverly worded reminders to our friends of their past offenses—you know, those unhappy keepsakes of the heart that reveal nothing more than how well we can carry a grudge.

Yeah, even Christians can be guilty of a spiritual disorder that could be called "petty syndrome."

But that's not God's way. If the Holy Spirit is in control of our lives, then He will help us to produce a fruit that is not hard or sour or rotten—but as sweet as heaven. We will produce love, joy, peace, patience, kindness, goodness, faithfulness. Now that is a way of life that can give us and everyone around us great joy as well as confidence in our walk with the Lord!

Holy Spirit, may the fruit I produce be as sweet and delicious as it is in heaven! Amen. —A.H.

Delight Yourself in the Lord!

Trust in the LORD, and do good; dwell in the land and
befriend faithfulness. Delight yourself in the LORD, and he
will give you the desires of your heart. Commit your
way to the LORD; trust in him, and he will act.

PSALM 37:3–5 ESV

"Delight yourself in the Lord" is a beautiful phrase, conjuring up all kinds of rapturous images, such as a wedding day full of every kind of pleasurable delicacy and sublime amusement and holy joy. But to delight oneself in the Lord, well, what would that look like exactly?

God wants us to create alongside Him, to not only use our many gifts to glorify Him but to know the paradisiacal bliss of being a cocreator with the Almighty. The Lord encourages us to luxuriate in the gifts of others too, such as attending a concert and being swept up in the euphoria of an exquisite piece of music. Or to commune with God throughout the day and find happiness in each other's company as two beloved friends. Also, God urges us to take pleasure in His glorious creation—like the splendor of a painted sunset, the wobbly dance of a newborn fawn, or the champagne laughter of children at play.

When it comes to the Lord, there is so much to delight in! Who can resist Him?

I love the way You light up the world, Lord,
with Your beauty and love! Amen. —A.H.

A Royal Pooh-Bah

*Do nothing from selfishness or empty conceit [through
factional motives, or strife], but with [an attitude of]
humility [being neither arrogant nor self-righteous],
regard others as more important than yourselves.*
PHILIPPIANS 2:3 AMP

There's too much wonderful stuff to do in this vast and ingenious world to fritter away our days and weeks. May we never get caught being a royal pooh-bah. God has given us too much to create, build, navigate, explore, and discover to ever waste our valuable time playing a fool on the world's stage. We need lots of good time for helping and healing and forgiving and loving and sharing and speaking words of life and blessing. . .you get the picture.

There should be no time left for spiritual junk that weighs down our souls—like being obnoxious or pretentious or pushy or arrogant. Like being gossipy, grumbly, or holding tightly to grudges. Like fretting or stirring up strife and fear, or being self-righteous or boastful or spiteful or crude. Remember, life is much too short to be a royal pooh-bah. It won't bring you confidence of any kind, and it sure won't win you any friends!

*Dear God, sometimes I act foolishly, and I am so sorry.
Please help me to regard others as more important
than myself. In Jesus' name I pray. Amen. —A.H.*

This Groaning Blue Ball

For we know that even the things of nature, like animals and plants, suffer in sickness and death as they await this great event. And even we Christians, although we have the Holy Spirit within us as a foretaste of future glory, also groan to be released from pain and suffering. We, too, wait anxiously for that day when God will give us our full rights as his children, including the new bodies he has promised us—bodies that will never be sick again and will never die.

ROMANS 8:22–23 TLB

We feel it every day. Every hour. Every minute. Our earth groans along with its inhabitants to be released from all the many moments of pain and suffering. When someone angrily cuts you off in traffic. When you fall on the unforgiving concrete. When that vacation money you saved up needs to go for unexpected medical bills. When a trusted coworker cheats you and then lies about it. When the church you love betrays you. When a lifelong friendship or marriage falls apart and reconciliation seems impossible.

Many times life seems hopeless. Yes, the world has cooked up a thousand and one ways to fix the problems, but as we can clearly see from man's failed attempts at salvation, there can be only one profoundly loving and perfectly lasting fix to all of it. . .Jesus Christ.

Lord, I am confident and excited about Your second coming. Come, Lord Jesus, come! Amen. —A.H.

Paradise Regained!

And He took the children [one by one] in His arms and blessed them
[with kind, encouraging words], placing His hands on them.

MARK 10:16 AMP

Some people think God is so far away they have no confidence in approaching Him or loving Him. But just as we show tenderness and affection for those we love, the Lord does too. If we love a child, we hold her in our arms and kiss her soft cheek. If we're crazy about our spouse, we might give him a special gift that will light up his world. If we care for our friends, we might be extra generous with our time.

When we read in the Bible about the Lord's devotion to us—how He wants to take each of us into His arms and tenderly and kindly speak to us, our response might be to burst into tears of joy. Why? Because humans long to connect to the One who made us—for paradise lost. We long for that intimate walk with God in the cool of the evening. Then to be assured in scripture of the depth of the Lord's love, well, it overwhelms us in the most delight-filled ways.

Yes, the Lord wants to take each of us, one by one, young or old, into His arms. How will you respond?

Jesus, someday we will meet face-to-face, but for now,
my spirit runs into Your arms where I know I am welcomed,
loved, and forever Yours. Amen. —A.H.

Always a Good Time

Let us then with confidence draw near to the throne of grace,
that we may receive mercy and find grace to help in time of need.
HEBREWS 4:16 ESV

Uh-oh. You just heard in the breakroom that your boss is in a foul mood, and he will spit nails at anyone who even thinks about coming into his office without a really good reason—like fire or imminent death. So maybe this isn't a good time to approach him about that much needed raise. Knowing him, though, you're not sure when a good time will ever be. Sigh.

That is not how we need to feel about approaching God. We can come to His throne of grace with confidence. We can receive mercy and grace in our time of need. We should always arrive with an attitude of respect, yes, but also with the sweet assurance of being loved by the Author of love. There will be no need for any sighs of disappointment or dread or dismissal.

When it comes to talking to God, now is always a good time.

Dear God, I come before You with so much on my mind, I'm not
sure where to begin. But I praise You and thank You that I can
come before You anytime day or night with the assurance of
Your love and mercy. In Jesus' name I pray. Amen. —A.H.

How Do We Live?

*Let no corrupting talk come out of your mouths, but only such
as is good for building up, as fits the occasion, that it may give
grace to those who hear. And do not grieve the Holy Spirit of
God, by whom you were sealed for the day of redemption.
Let all bitterness and wrath and anger and clamor and
slander be put away from you, along with all malice.*

EPHESIANS 4:29–31 ESV

Sometimes humans look a bit like those robotic vacuum cleaners that
keep going around and around the room bumping into things. Maybe
they do clean up the floor to a degree, but they always have that random,
bumblebee-thumping-on-the-window look. When heaven sees the way
we live, is that how we look as we go around and around trying to live out
our story—bumbling randomly and never really taking care of the mess?

As Christians, we don't have to live haphazardly. The Bible gives
us excellent advice, and Ephesians is a part of that wisdom for living a
redemptive life in Christ that changes not only our story on earth but
also guarantees us an epilogue with a heavenly ending!

*Lord, I admit I'm tired of trying a hit-and-miss
way of living. Please guide me in all things with
the power of Your holy Word. Amen. —A.H.*

The Real You

Where shall I go from your Spirit?
Or where shall I flee from your presence?
If I ascend to heaven, you are there!
If I make my bed in Sheol, you are there!
If I take the wings of the morning
and dwell in the uttermost parts of the sea,
even there your hand shall lead me.
PSALM 139:7–10 ESV

Admit it—we would be ashamed if people could see certain pieces of our private lives. What if (unknown to us) there was a mini-cam following us around, and some select scenes of our interactions with people showed up on social media? It might even go viral. Oh dear. Would people smile and cheer or would they cringe, knowing now that our smiles were as fake as a bowl of plastic fruit and our deeds were as empty as an upside-down bucket? Sigh.

Even if our deeds and thoughts can be hidden from people, God is watching everything, and this includes our entire thought-life. We can try, but we cannot flee from God's presence. That is the good news that keeps us humble, and that is the good news that reminds us of His caring attentions.

May we live so guilelessly and winsomely as Christians that people will be so happily surprised that they will be open to hearing the good news of Christ!

Lord, please make the real me into someone beautiful inside and
out, and then show me how to move forward with confidence
as I reach out to others in Your name. Amen. —A.H.

Just Can't Be Still

Oh sing to the LORD a new song;
sing to the LORD, all the earth!
Sing to the LORD, bless his name;
tell of his salvation from day to day.
Declare his glory among the nations,
his marvelous works among all the peoples!
For great is the LORD, and greatly to be praised;
he is to be feared above all gods.

PSALM 96:1–4 ESV

The music is good. Mmm. So good. And you want to spin and sway and laugh with joy. But you have to sit. Okay, so for now you sit, but you can't help but let your foot wiggle in time with the music. The elation and pleasure and praise of it all have to come out somewhere!

Have you even known life to be so full that your heart wanted to cry out in joy? You wanted to cheer or raise your hands or dance before the Lord like David did? You wanted to sing a new song that has never been sung before? Not for an audience but for God alone? Then do so. With gusto. With your whole heart and soul. We as Christians have good reason to rejoice. We should not always be still but be filled with animation and adoration to declare the Lord's glory and His marvelous works, for He is worthy of our devotion, our reverence, and yes, our songs of praise!

Lord, I want to sing a new song just for You.
Please show me how! Amen. —A.H.

Overcoming!

*"I have said these things to you, that in me you may
have peace. In the world you will have tribulation.
But take heart; I have overcome the world."*

JOHN 16:33 ESV

To be a Christian woman of confidence seems to be the last thing hoped for when you're just trying to make it through another long day. You're up early to make school lunches. Then off to work. Bleary-eyed, you suffer through another day at the office. Then after heavy traffic home, you conjure up dinner from boxes of this and that, tidy the house, and drop into bed. As exhausted as you are, you ruminate half the night over all the cruel comments on social media and all the horrors from the evening news!

How can there be confidence when the whole world is coming unglued and you can barely make it through another day?

Yes, the world is full of tribulation, but Christ has overcome it all. We can have confidence in His power to help us, to sustain us, and to bring us peace. But we do need to do our part by learning the art of sweet rest with the Lord on the Sabbath, to eat healthy foods, to know when to delegate, and when to unplug from social media, the news, the internet, and our phones. Confidence comes more easily when we do life God's way!

*Lord, I want You to show me a new way to live—
in peace, hope, and confidence. Amen. —A.H.*

That's How It's Done

Never tire of loyalty and kindness. Hold these
virtues tightly. Write them deep within your heart.
PROVERBS 3:3 TLB

The line is long, the cashier is lollygagging, and you're going to be late for your doctor's appointment. You want to blast the woman with a few choice words—maybe even give her the evil eye—but you know that in the end the harshness will ruin her day and yours. So you pray for her. And you pray for *you* too. Instead of a verbal thrashing, you choose to calmly mention your situation to her and hope that she has mercy.

When life is cruising along nicely, kindness is easy to pull off, right? But put a kink in the day, and one might become desperate to get life flowing again. A desire for personal convenience can undermine one's good intentions.

Yeah, sometimes kindness isn't easy. Sometimes it requires sacrifice. Proverbs reminds us not to tire of loyalty and kindness. That we should hold these virtues tightly and even write them deep within our hearts.

Will these virtues always be easy? No, but when we follow through—when we truly get it right—we can almost hear God say, *"Now that's how it's done!"*

Dear Lord, show me how to be a woman of
kindness even when it isn't easy. Amen. —A.H.

When Hope Seems Lost

*The Lord is close to the brokenhearted
and saves those who are crushed in spirit.*

PSALM 34:18

Some days are harder than others. The world and its tribulations can weigh on us heavily. Personal suffering of every kind can come suddenly and overwhelm our spirits until it feels like all the light and hope has been consumed by the darkness. We may come to believe that even God has given up on us. But that can never be the case. Psalm 147:3 reminds us, "He heals the brokenhearted and binds up their wounds."

When you feel like giving up, know how deeply the Lord cares for you. You can cry out to Him, any hour of any day. Remember too that in Jeremiah 29:11, we are told, " 'For I know the plans I have for you,' declares the Lord, 'plans to prosper you and not to harm you, plans to give you hope and a future.' "

And miraculously, God can also help you with the wise assistance of good Christian counselors and the comforting words of a compassionate and trusted friend.

Dear God, I cry out to You in my time of need. I feel so brokenhearted and overwhelmed by life. Please strengthen me. Please mend my heart and fill me with hope. In Jesus' name I pray. Amen. —A.H.

Some Jolly in Your Step

A tranquil heart gives life to the flesh,
but envy makes the bones rot.
PROVERBS 14:30 ESV

Have you been caught thinking any of the following: *If only I had more square footage in my house like my best friend. If only my hair were more colored and coiffed like my coworker. Or maybe I need a few of her cute outfits. She always looks so put-together and accessorized while I look like I've been dragged behind a bus!* Or on a more spiritual level, maybe you feel all your Christian friends were given more godly gifts and dazzling talents because God loves them more.

The moment we choose to do those envious comparison studies with others, we veer off from our own unique life-journey and we start jolliping—but with very little jolly—down a foreign path. We are sure to stumble again and again. We must keep our focus on what God has for us; that is, our one-of-a-kind mission using the distinctive gifts and talents He has given us. When we walk closely with the Lord on the path He has created for us, confidence will come. We can walk with surefootedness, our hearts will be more tranquil, and there will be a bit of jolly in our step too!

I love the way You made me, Lord. Please help
me to stop comparing myself to others. Amen. —A.H.

When the Miracle Doesn't Come

*And he withdrew from them about a stone's throw, and knelt down
and prayed, saying, "Father, if you are willing, remove this cup from
me. Nevertheless, not my will, but yours, be done."*
LUKE 22:41–42 ESV

You've prayed. You've fasted. You wait, believing, but nothing happens.
We know God wants us to bring our requests to Him and to have faith
that He will give us what we need, but when no miracle comes, what
then? It's helpful to remember Jesus' prayer before His death and resurrection. Even though He hoped for a way out of what was to come,
in the end, Jesus said to His Father in heaven, "Not my will, but yours,
be done."

We can't help but wonder, "What if God had answered the prayer of
Jesus and He hadn't paid the price for our sins?" That question makes
us sorrowful and perplexed, but it also fills us with gratitude for how the
prayer was answered. Yes, sometimes God says yes to us, but sometimes
He says no with a greater plan in mind—one that we perhaps cannot
understand until later.

When it comes to God, though, glory always happens. And in the
matter of Jesus' prayer in the garden, well, a miracle did arrive for all of
us—the miracle of redemption.

*Lord, remind me of Your willing sacrifice when I pray for my needs.
May I always end my requests as You did, "Your will be done." —A.H.*

Beautiful to Behold

*"So, every healthy tree bears good fruit,
but the diseased tree bears bad fruit."*

MATTHEW 7:17 ESV

That apricot you plucked off your grandmother's tree looks like pure ambrosia. You bite into it, and the juicy nectar runs down your chin. The taste of it makes you squeal, "Oolala!" It's fully ripened, sweet as candy, and usable for all good things—like your granny's homemade preserves. What a treat. What a joy. Yes, oh yes, this is the way a tree and its fruit are meant to be.

From reading this verse in Matthew, we need to ask ourselves if the fruit we produce is as beautiful to behold as that apricot. Is it a welcomed delight? Or would our lives be described as something quite different? Perhaps a bit withered and spoiled in a few places because the tree itself became sickly from the many contaminates of the world?

The good news is that God can make our fruit what it should be, so that people will be pleased we showed up. They will listen to us with anticipation. They will be glad to know us—honorable women of conviction, of inner beauty and integrity.

*Dear God, even if I need Your holy hand to prune me with
correction, I am willing. Please make me into good fruit that
is usable in Your kingdom. In Jesus' name I pray. Amen. —A.H.*

The World Is Upright Again

If you love someone, you will be loyal to him no matter what the cost. You will always believe in him, always expect the best of him, and always stand your ground in defending him.

1 Corinthians 13:7 TLB

When a person is floundering around in life like a woman on skates who has no idea how to skate—arms flailing and mouth open wide—it's hard to deal with humanity, even those we may love dearly. It is easier to doubt people, give up on them, think the worst of them, or generally abandon them even when they need us the most.

But that is not what Christ expects of us.

If we are confident of who we are in Christ, we can officially calm down. The world is upright again. We can breathe. Smell the lilacs. Smile awhile. Rest in Him. And then we can focus on good things like truth and loyalty and loving people as Christ has loved us.

Lord, sometimes I jump to conclusions about people, even family and friends. I judge and criticize and act in ways that I know displease You. Please help me to always be confident in You so that I can reflect that assurance and goodness to the rest of the world. Amen. —A.H.

The Love of My Life

And I pray that Christ will be more and more at home in your hearts, living within you as you trust in him. May your roots go down deep into the soil of God's marvelous love; and may you be able to feel and understand, as all God's children should, how long, how wide, how deep, and how high his love really is; and to experience this love for yourselves, though it is so great that you will never see the end of it or fully know or understand it. And so at last you will be filled up with God himself.

EPHESIANS 3:17–19 TLB

Have you ever fallen head over heels in love? Many people have, and it's a beautiful thing. You long to be near to your sweetheart and to know every little detail—such as what brings sorrow or joy to your beloved.

As we get to know God, we may find something similar happening to us. That we long to be near Him, to know all the things that bring Him sorrow or joy. Yes, somewhere along the way, the relationship moved from feelings of obligation, work, and fear to thinking, *I want to be with the Lord and work with Him out of love and gratitude. He is the love of my life!*

Lord, the more I know of You, the more I love You dearly! Amen. —A.H.

Beautiful Lighting Effects

"You are the light of the world. A city set on a hill cannot be hidden. Nor do people light a lamp and put it under a basket, but on a stand, and it gives light to all in the house. In the same way, let your light shine before others, so that they may see your good works and give glory to your Father who is in heaven."

MATTHEW 5:14–16 ESV

People are enamored with lighting effects. You can create so many beautiful effects at work and at home, even at church, with every kind of combination of color, intensity, placement, and style. What fun. Maybe you are one of the floodlight folks or the moody-glow people or even one of those golden-vintage-bulb souls. But whatever kind of light we are gifted to shine, it must always illuminate the one true God.

Yes, because of our good works and moral excellence, we can—with joy and confidence—become the beautiful lighting effects meant to illuminate Christ. How can you be that irresistible light in a dark world?

Dear God, I don't want to hide my light under a basket but put it on a stand to give light for all to see. Please show me the many ways I can shine for You and bring You glory! In Jesus' name I pray. Amen. —A.H

A Helping Hand

But if anyone has the world's goods and sees his brother in need, yet closes his heart against him, how does God's love abide in him?

1 John 3:17 esv

Sometimes when we're zooming to church to get there on time, are we in too big a toot to help the woman on the street who is clearly homeless? Or do we deliberately glance away so as not to see her at all? But if we repeatedly ignore the cries of the poor, how do we have the love of God in us? You may think, *Well, I have little to give.* But Jesus is even more impressed with us when we give out of our slim funds than if we give out of bounty. After all, it is easy to be a generous benefactor when we are only skimming a bit off the top of our wealth.

May we as Christians be the ones who not only see the poor but also become well known for our compassion and generosity. May the love of God pour from us freely as we help and give and as we encourage people with the most reassuring news this world will ever hear—that Jesus has come to offer mercy, love, and grace.

Lord, may my heart always be full of compassion for those who are in need. Amen. —A.H.

The Sweet Air of Forever

For the Lord himself will come down from heaven, with a loud command, with the voice of the archangel and with the trumpet call of God, and the dead in Christ will rise first. After that, we who are still alive and are left will be caught up together with them in the clouds to meet the Lord in the air. And so we will be with the Lord forever.

1 THESSALONIANS 4:16–17

As followers of Christ, we will someday be with the Lord forever. That last word—*forever*—makes us pause, doesn't it? Such wonderful news, and yet it's impossible to comprehend eternity since we live inside Earth's finite framework. This very limited commodity has become paramount to us, influencing every aspect of our lives. We crave more and more of it, but there will be closure.

The good news for lovers of Christ is that heaven will know no end. There will be freedom to enjoy life in all its richness. We will come to know the Lord better with perfect fellowship. There will be time to use our gifts to their fullest and discover new talents as well. In all we do, there will be no need to scurry, hurry, hustle, bustle, rush, or dash. We will breathe the sweet air of forever.

Lord, I thank You that as Your child, I have the beautiful confidence of someday being in heaven with You for all time. Amen. —A.H.

Trust in God—Not Your Gut

If you want favor with both God and man, and a reputation for
good judgment and common sense, then trust the Lord completely;
don't ever trust yourself. In everything you do, put God first,
and he will direct you and crown your efforts with success.

PROVERBS 3:5–6 TLB

There is a popular saying these days to "just go with your gut." But as upbeat and rational as it sounds, what does that phrase really mean? Is it wisdom or folly? Going with our gut might be another way to say that we just want what we want when we want it. That kind of self-centered philosophy is some of the thinking that got mankind into trouble in the first place.

Adam and Eve liked the idea of being like God and basically doing life any way they chose to. We are made in God's image, but we are *not* God. Big difference. And that difference is important, since God made us, not the other way around. We are the creatures not the Creator, and He knows best.

So when making big life decisions, little ones, and everything in between, trust God for it all, not your gut. The Lord promises not only to guide us but also to crown our efforts with success!

Holy Spirit, guide me in all areas of my life. I give
You permission to be in full control. Amen. —A.H.

So Not a Good Look

*But the LORD said to Samuel, "Do not look on his appearance
or on the height of his stature, because I have rejected him.
For the LORD sees not as man sees: man looks on the outward
appearance, but the LORD looks on the heart."*

1 SAMUEL 16:7 ESV

You finally slow down long enough to take a real assessing look in a
full-length mirror, and you are mortified at the way you've let your appearance go. You look anything but well groomed and professional.
Maybe you could upgrade your look a bit.

But what if you finally get that fab new look, and you don't bother
to get a makeover on your heart? Hmm. So how do you think people
see you? As a little untrustworthy, or sneaky, or whiny, stingy, fearful,
cranky, gossipy, or one who stirs up trouble? Maybe a friend at work
sees you lambaste an intern and then quietly says to you, "Honey, that
is so not a good look on you." Uh-oh. Maybe it's time to take another
long look in the mirror. Yes, by all means, groom the body, but first let
God groom your soul.

*Dear Lord, I'd like to upgrade my spiritual life. Help me to
be faithful in my prayer time, in attending Your house of
worship, and in reading Your Word. Amen. —A.H.*

What Tomorrow Will Bring

Come now, you who say, "Today or tomorrow we will go into such and such a town and spend a year there and trade and make a profit"—yet you do not know what tomorrow will bring. What is your life? For you are a mist that appears for a little time and then vanishes. Instead you ought to say, "If the Lord wills, we will live and do this or that."

JAMES 4:13–15 ESV

You can't wait for your vacation in Greece. In fact, you can't stop talking about every little detail of your meticulously laid plans. Or perhaps you've been promised a raise and promotion, so you buy a house to celebrate what you know will come.

God wants us to be happy, and He loves to give us good gifts, but sometimes we place our confidence in the wrong things. In our own abilities. In the promises of other people. In our degrees and accolades or our family heritage. In our good looks perhaps. Maybe in our reputations or fortunes.

Any one of those blessings could vanish like the wind, and then where would we be? Even though we make grand plans, long-term goals, and sweeping pronouncements, we don't know what tomorrow will bring. To please God is to put our confidence in Him by saying, "If the Lord wills, we will live and do this or that."

Lord, I'm sorry that I make big plans without You.
Please forgive me. Amen. —A.H.

A Touch of Kindness

Instead, you must worship Christ as Lord of your life. And if someone asks about your hope as a believer, always be ready to explain it.
1 PETER 3:15 NLT

Okay, you understand the importance of witnessing, but what if no one ever asks you about your life with Christ? Well, if you hide your faith like you're embarrassed about it, she won't ask. If you act like a buffoon, she won't ask. If you act like you don't give a flying fig about her life—by talking nonstop about yourself, your new tires, your unruly kids, your recent vacation, your chipped nails—she won't ask. You get the picture, bright and clear.

However, she might ask you about your faith if you show her a touch of kindness. If you listen with your heart, not a pretend "listen" with a nod and a smile, but truly listen to hear and learn and care, then she will come a lot closer to asking you what you care about and what you believe. Then the door may open and the time may come to tell her about your hope and what Christ has done in your life.

Holy Spirit, teach me how to be Your ambassador,
loving people as You do. Help me to know when
to speak up and when to be quiet! Amen. —A.H.

A Beautiful Calling

*"For who is greater, the one who is at the table
or the one who serves? Is it not the one who is at
the table? But I am among you as one who serves."*

LUKE 22:27

A vinegary kind of a woman throws open the doors of the banquet hall and nearly knocks people down as she marches toward the head table. You quickly step aside since you can plainly see that she is a force to be reckoned with. After being seated, the woman proceeds to order the staff around and hold her nose high enough to catch flies.

The world preaches this sermon to each of us—that in life we are to always strive for head table status. That we should even expect it, because we deserve it. But no matter the clever and enticing lectures of the world, that is not the way of heaven. Not the way Christ personally showed us how to deal with our fellow man.

Philippians 2:7 (NLT) tells us, "Instead, he gave up his divine privileges; he took the humble position of a slave and was born as a human being."

There's certainly nothing wrong with being asked to sit at the head of the table at a banquet as long as we remember that servanthood is a beautiful calling for all of us.

Holy Spirit, show me how to have a servant's heart. Amen. —A.H.

A Good Night's Sleep

But I say to you, love [that is, unselfishly seek the best or higher good for] your enemies and pray for those who persecute you.
MATTHEW 5:44 AMP

You wake up at 2:34 a.m., and then you toss and turn. You start thinking about every little thing. And big things. Like the person who has taken an intense dislike to you at work just because you're a Christian. Or the cruel comments on social media that you can't get out of your head. Or all the people you once admired on TV who are now shaking their fists in red-faced rages. In fact, you worry that the whole world has gone mad! In other words, you are not going to get back to sleep tonight. Now what?

Pray for them—with confidence in the Lord's supernatural power. Pray for all of them. The people who hate you. The people who persecute you. The people who shake their fists and spew the cruelest of words.

Then somehow in all that clean wash of purifying prayer, God will show you how you can love them. And in that glimmer of love, you may get some good sleep after all. Nighty night. . .

Lord, my heart has been so unhappy, thinking of all the bitterness and brokenness around me. Please show me how to love in a world that seems bent on hate. Amen. —A.H.

An Overthrow of Sin

But thanks be to God, who gives us the victory
[as conquerors] through our Lord Jesus Christ.
1 CORINTHIANS 15:57 AMP

The Zealots during Bible times had hoped that Jesus had come to overthrow the Romans, but Christ came with a very different agenda. He wanted to overthrow sin and death, not the Roman Empire. He came not to change the government but to change the human heart. And that is exactly what He accomplished.

Perhaps people think it's easier to start a revolution than to acknowledge a revelation—that is, "I am a sinner and in great need of a Savior." Humanity has always been offended by the Gospel, and yet it is humanity that has done the offending against God with a malicious and mutinous heart. We want to blame everyone else for the world's anarchy, and yet the anarchy stirs within our own souls.

Simply put, pride gets in the way of what we need most—repentance. When we submit to Christ, though, freedom comes. As Christians we should wave a flag of victory!

Dear God, forgive me for my rebellion, and please set me
free from the bondage of sin. May I always raise a flag of
victory in Your name because You have conquered sin
and death! In Jesus' name I pray. Amen. —A.H.

Getting Ahead of God

Now Sarai, Abram's wife, had borne him no children. But she had an
Egyptian slave named Hagar; so she said to Abram, "The Lord has
kept me from having children. Go, sleep with my slave; perhaps I
can build a family through her." Abram agreed to what Sarai said.

GENESIS 16:1–2

You prayed—again—and still you wait. You believe God is on your side, but you're also thinking, *I need help now. I think I'll give God some assistance. Maybe He's too busy with world affairs. Perhaps He forgot His promises. Maybe I don't have the close relationship with the Lord as I had hoped for.*

We're all guilty of getting ahead of the Lord because we don't like His timing. That is what Abraham and Sarah did long ago. If you read the full biblical passage of Abraham and Sarah (beginning with Genesis 16) and how they refused to wait for God's promise to give them a son, you will see the disastrous results of such an action. Their disobedience had a negative ripple effect through time, and our choices outside the Lord's leading will have an undesirable effect too. That is why putting our full confidence in God's plan and His timing is paramount to pleasing Him and vital to a life well lived!

Holy Spirit, guide me in all things, and teach me
to wait on Your timing, not mine. Amen. —A.H.

Your Dumpling Darling

My child, don't reject the Lord's discipline,
and don't be upset when he corrects you.
For the Lord corrects those he loves,
just as a father corrects a child in whom he delights.
PROVERBS 3:11–12 NLT

No matter the stern lectures, a child may still yank her hand away and race out into the busy street. A good parent may shriek, chase, grab her hand, scoop her up, and then hug the little gal until she can barely breathe. But then comes the discipline so that such dangerous and potentially deadly disobedience never happens again. Why the chastisement? Because she is your dumpling darling, your treasure. Only a good parent would make certain to teach a child about what is right and wrong, what is dangerous and safe, and then wisely scold when they deliberately disobey.

Only a loving God would do the same. When we choose to deliberately disobey our Lord, there will be a reprimand and perhaps some humbling consequences. But would we really want it any other way? As it says in Proverbs 15:5 (NLT), "Only a fool despises a parent's discipline; whoever learns from correction is wise."

Dear God, may I never run from Your loving discipline. May
I always embrace the correction, learn from it, and move
forward with wiser steps. In Jesus' name I pray. Amen. —A.H.

Confidence in Giving

*Let each one give [thoughtfully and with purpose]
just as he has decided in his heart, not grudgingly or
under compulsion, for God loves a cheerful giver
[and delights in the one whose heart is in his gift].*

2 CORINTHIANS 9:7 AMP

There is need everywhere. The church asks for offerings to share the Gospel overseas or to dig water wells in foreign countries. The local food pantry is low and puts out a request for donations. The homeless woman on the street holds up a sign, asking for help. There are countless ministries all around the world that perform many noble and godly deeds and that also need financial assistance.

Feeling a bit overwhelmed? So what is a compassionate Christian to do? God shows us in His Word how to handle the fine art of giving. First we thoughtfully and prayerfully decide in our heart what is right for us to give. Then once the amounts and people or ministries are determined, we should not do it with reluctance. We should not do it begrudgingly. We should do it with an open hand and a merry spirit. Why? Because God loves a cheerful giver, which is just the way He gives to us!

*Lord, give me wisdom when I give,
and help me to do it happily! Amen. —A.H.*

Canceling the Wedding

Before you Gentiles knew God, you were slaves to so-called gods that do not even exist. So now that you know God (or should I say, now that God knows you), why do you want to go back again and become slaves once more to the weak and useless spiritual principles of this world?

GALATIANS 4:8–9 NLT

Only one week until your wedding day, and it will be the best day of your life. You and your beloved are so in love you wonder if two hearts can even contain such joy. But for some reason you start to listen to the wrong people, or you allow confusion and fear to taint your joy. Then in one life-altering moment, you choose to throw your gorgeous wedding gown into a dumpster, and you cancel the wedding.

We almost shudder to think of such an event, since we don't want anyone to give up something so beautiful, so wonderful, so perfect. But that scene helps to illustrate what Paul was saying to the Galatians when they became Christians and then wanted to go back to the way things were. Paul asked, "Why do you want to go back again and become slaves once more to the weak and useless spiritual principles of this world?"

Why indeed. . .

Lord, may I never be so enticed by the world that I choose its useless principles over You and Your beautiful and wonderful and perfect ways! Amen. —A.H.

A Walk with God

The Lord is my shepherd;
I have all that I need.
He lets me rest in green meadows;
he leads me beside peaceful streams.
He renews my strength.
He guides me along right paths,
bringing honor to his name.

PSALM 23:1–3 NLT

We like to think we're invincible—that we can work mindlessly and tirelessly like robots, but as flesh and blood and spirit, we require rest. Period. Otherwise we will short-out our wires from exhaustion. The inner workings and influences and outright demands of the world can change our priorities and cause us to push when we need to pray or pause. What if the enemy can keep us so weary that we are of no use to God's kingdom?

We can't go out into the world with confidence when we're dragging our feet like a whiny toddler who's trying to dodge a much-needed nap! We won't be fresh to share the Good News or bring honor to the Lord's name when we're frazzled from too much social media, TV, and techno gadgets. We will inevitably become ineffectual. As your Shepherd, the Lord longs to lead you by still waters and those gentle green pastures for a rest. Allow Him to renew your strength. See just how wonderful and renewing a walk with God can be.

Lead me by still waters, Lord. I am so weary
and ready to follow You! Amen. —A.H.

All in the Name of Love

"As the Father has loved me, so have I loved you.
Now remain in my love."

JOHN 15:9

Someone's child is out on the baseball field and warming up to throw a pitch. But he seems distracted and scans the bleachers, most likely looking for any sign of his parents. None to be seen, he sighs. He looks scared—maybe shaking in his little cleats—and almost ready to run when his parents arrive at the back. They smile big and cheer him on with waves and shouts. The boy lights up like the sun above them.

The boy would be just fine now. He just needed to know that the people he cared about most in the world had shown up. Someone to support his efforts, to cheer him on. To be there for him, all in the name of love.

Be confident. God showed up for us—the One who cares more for us than anyone else in the world—and He sent His Son to die for us . . .all in the name of love.

Dear God, I thank You that You loved me so much that You sent Your Son, Jesus, to live among us and to die for my sins and the sins of the world. I love You, Lord. Amen. —A.H.

When the World Chips Away

If you are insulted because of the name of Christ,
you are blessed, for the Spirit of glory and of God rests on you.
1 PETER 4:14

The persecution of God's people usually makes us conjure up images of severe oppressions endured in some faraway land, but in America we're seeing more and more Christians being ridiculed, tormented, fired from their jobs, and made fun of for their faith. Some of these insults are not whispered behind our backs but brazenly declared on TV, social media, movies, and in almost every other area of our society.

We don't like to think that we might be harassed for our faith, but considering today's rising anti-Christian atmosphere, we can expect to be discriminated against, intimidated, or abused in some way if we are open about our walk with the Lord.

When the powers of darkness in this world chip away at our confidence in Christ, be of good courage. When we are insulted because of the name of Christ, we are blessed, for the Spirit of glory and of God rests on us! We can stand tall in that truth and remain confident in our faith.

Lord, please give me the strength to endure the world's
persecution. Help me not to hate those who torment
me but love them as You do. Amen. —A.H.

The Mighty Power of God

For this reason I remind you to fan into flame the gift of God, which is in you through the laying on of my hands, for God gave us a spirit not of fear but of power and love and self-control. Therefore do not be ashamed of the testimony about our Lord, nor of me his prisoner, but share in suffering for the gospel by the power of God.

2 TIMOTHY 1:6–8 ESV

Our culture is enthralled by superheroes. We like to watch them on the silver screen, buy the paraphernalia, and perhaps even pretend we're one of them. We would all like to think we could sweep in and do noble deeds like stop a thief or rescue a child. We may not have the ability to fly through the air or spring across buildings, but as Christians, God does give us supernatural power to do His will on this earth. We are not to tiptoe out into the world with a timid or fearful mind-set but with the assurance that we can do all things through Christ who gives us strength (see Philippians 4:13).

May we all go forth each day with confidence not in our own abilities but in the mighty power of the great God we serve.

Lord, please stir in me the desire to go out into the world, knowing well that You didn't give me a spirit of fear but of power and love and self-control. In Jesus' name I pray. Amen. —A.H.

Until we meet again,
we would like to leave you
with this ancient and beautiful Irish blessing:

May the road rise to meet you.
May the wind be always at your back.
May the sun shine warm upon your face.
And rains fall soft upon your fields.
And until we meet again,
May God hold you in
the palm of His hand.

Bestselling and award-winning author **Anita Higman** has fifty books published. She's been a Barnes & Noble "Author of the Month" for Houston and has a BA in the combined fields of speech communication, psychology, and art.

A few of Anita's favorite things are fairy-tale castles; steampunk clothes; traveling around Europe; exotic teas like orchid, heather, and wild blueberry; romantic movies; laughing around the dinner table with family and friends; and gardening—although most of the time she has no idea what she's doing!

Feel free to drop by Anita's website at www.anitahigman.com or connect with her on her Facebook reader page at www.facebook.com/AuthorAnitaHigman. She would love to hear from you!

Author, editor, and speaker **Judy Gordon Morrow** has published a dozen nonfiction books, along with articles, poetry, and song lyrics. God surprised her by turning her prayer journals into a daily devotional book, *The Listening Heart: Hearing God in Prayer*. A lifelong lover of words, Judy has served as a school librarian, newspaper copyeditor, and nonfiction editor at Multnomah Publishers.

Always an avid reader, Judy collects books old and new and combines them with vintage and whimsy to create a cozy home that invites smiles. She delights in trying new recipes, walking at sunset, arranging flowers, singing hymns, watching heart-tugging movies, and indulging in dark chocolate.

Judy treasures her family and friends and relishes rich conversations around her kitchen table or wherever she goes. She'd love to connect with you at her website, www.judygordonmorrow.com, or on her Facebook author page at www.facebook.com/JudyGordonMorrow/.

CONTINUE TO LET GOD GROW YOUR FAITH!

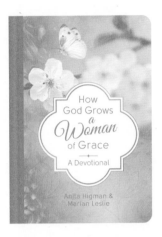

How God Grows a Woman of Grace

How God Grows a Woman of Grace is designed to
enhance a woman's spiritual journey. Featuring two
hundred–plus devotional readings complemented by
scripture selections and prayers, this lovely collection
offers a powerful blend of inspiration, encouragement,
and grace for every area of a woman's life.

Hardback / 978-1-68322-782-3 / $12.99